THE FURTHERANCE OF THE NEW WAY FOR THE LORD'S RECOVERY

WITNESS LEE

Living Stream Ministry
Anaheim, CA

First Edition, June 2001.

ISBN 0-7363-1282-X

Published by

Living Stream Ministry
2431 W. La Palma Ave., Anaheim, CA 92801 U.S.A.
P. O. Box 2121, Anaheim, CA 92814 U.S.A.

Printed in the United States of America

01 02 03 04 05 06 07 / 10 9 8 7 6 5 4 3 2 1

CONTENTS

PREFACE

This book is a translation of messages given in Chinese by Brother Witness Lee in Taipei, Taiwan in the winter of 1986. It contains seven chapters, beginning with a definition of the Lord's recovery and its new way and continuing with a discussion of the commission and definite steps for the carrying out of the new way and the key to its success. This is truly an indispensable guide for the advancement, increase, and spread of the churches. These messages were not reviewed by the speaker.

CHAPTER ONE

THE SPECIFIC COORDINATION OF THE CHURCHES FOR PRACTICING THE NEW WAY

Scripture Reading: Luke 19:9; Acts 10:22-24; 16:13-15, 29-34; 18:8; Rom. 16:3-5; 1 Cor. 1:16; 16:19; Col. 4:15; Philem. 2; Heb. 11:7; 2 Pet. 2:5

When we speak about the furtherance of the new way for the Lord's recovery, we mean that the only goal of our practicing the new way is to promote the Lord's recovery.

THE MOVE OF THE LORD'S RECOVERY

What is known as the Lord's recovery began at the latest in the Reformation, which took place in the sixteenth century through Martin Luther. Actually before that time, even in the years A.D. 200 through 300, the Lord's recovery was already in existence. During that time, there were small groups of people, one after another, who saw that the church of their day had become deformed. Thus, they had a strong burden and hope in the depths of their heart and spirit to bring the church back to its earliest condition. This was the beginning of the recovery. Throughout the ages this flow of recovery has not stopped. At the beginning of this century the flow turned from the West and went to China. In 1922 the first church in the Lord's recovery in China was started in Foochow, which was Brother Nee's hometown. It has been sixty-four years since that time, and in all those years the Lord moved in many ways in His recovery while simultaneously releasing much truth and light.

Like the other works of the Lord, His recovery is carried out through His word and follows His word, which is the truth. According to church history, the most important accomplishment of the saints who had begun to pay attention to the Lord's recovery in the second and third centuries was the recovery of the truth, the Lord's word. When the Lord raised up the recovery among us in China, we did not do anything apart from this matter. We just sought to know the truth and to understand the Lord's speaking. The Bible clearly shows us that God's work is accomplished through His speaking. As soon as He speaks, His move is brought in. Without His speaking, He does not move. Not only is the work of the new creation carried out in this way; even the work of the old creation—the creation of the heavens, the earth, and all things—was accomplished through God's speaking. The New Testament tells us that all creation came into being, or was produced, through God's word (Heb. 1:2-3; John 1:3; 2 Pet. 3:5). God's word is the truth. This is a very important matter.

The primary leading one of the Lord's recovery in China was Brother Watchman Nee, who had the notable characteristic of being able to see the light of the truth and to recover the way of truth. From that time on, the Lord has never stopped recovering the light of the truth among us. Later I was sent out from mainland China, and it can be said that the recovery of the Lord's truth has been even stronger than before. In these past twenty years, especially after the spread of the Lord's recovery to the West, the Lord's light and truth have been pouring out like a waterfall. The books we publish are far richer in content and greater in number than ever before. For this reason, much of the Lord's move has been brought forth.

The Lord's move does not depend merely on the truth; it depends even more on the vitality of the truth, which is life. In the Lord's move, if there is only the truth yet the people themselves are deadened and not living, then everything is still empty. Hence, whenever the Lord reveals and releases the truth, action will follow, and the vitality within the action is life. We can all see one fact: On the one hand, we must confess that we are feeble and small, short of knowledge, and weak in the testimony we live out; yet, on the other hand, we see that if we compare the Lord's recovery of the light of the truth and the condition of life among us with what is found among the majority of today's Christians, we can only bow our heads to worship and thank the Lord that due to His great mercy we have truly advanced in the matters of truth and life.

For the past twenty years my work has been carried out mainly in the West, and most of my writings have been written in English. The most up-to-date vision has recently been published in the book *God's New Testament Economy*. That book consists of forty-four chapters, of which the last nineteen chapters deal exclusively with the New Jerusalem. We can now say that the New Jerusalem is the greatest, most consummate truth in the Bible. Furthermore, not long ago we published seven new books. Among them, three speak mainly about the way of promoting the Lord's recovery, while the other four are a collection of messages I gave over the past twenty years in America. Although it has been almost a quarter of a century, those messages are still fresh, living, and full of supply. This is the sweet, wonderful grace bestowed on us by the Lord.

THE LACK IN THE LORD'S RECOVERY TODAY

In summary, we can say that the truth among us today is unprecedented in richness. Comparatively speaking, we are at a high point in the matter of life. However, we still have a great lack because after sixty-four years, the number of people in the Lord's recovery is not very large. By His mercy, from the time the Lord's recovery began in China until 1949 when we left the mainland, there were gatherings in the Lord's recovery in all thirty-five provinces, but the number of people was not so great. After coming to Taiwan we labored industriously for twelve years. From 1960 to 1962, when the Lord brought us to the Western world, the work of the Lord's recovery also entered into the English-speaking world. Through the convenient geographical position of the United States and the widespread use of the English language, in more than twenty years the Lord's recovery has spread from the United States to the other four continents. Originally the recovery was confined to Asia. Then it went to North America, and from there it has spread to South America, Europe, Africa, and Australia.

According to the calculation we made a few years ago,

there are more than six hundred churches on the six continents of the globe. This number is not small, but it is not large either. With respect to the number in the meetings, it is still too small; on average, each locality has only two hundred people in the meetings. Thus, the total number of people in all the churches is about 120,000. A great part of these people are in Taiwan, because Taiwan alone has more than forty thousand, or one-third of the entire number. In the other localities most of the meetings have fifty to sixty people, others have twenty to thirty, and still others have about one hundred. There are not many localities that have reached two hundred or more. This is a great lack in the Lord's recovery today, and it is something which we pay particular attention to in the move of the Lord's recovery in the new way.

In the last sixty years, the truth in the Lord's recovery has not been lacking, and even though our life has not been quite so rich, it is still adequate. There is only one matter which has really become a problem—the matter of increase and spread. According to the truth which the Lord has shown us and according to the life which He has given to us, our increase and spread are too poor. This is especially true of the ten years from 1974 to 1984 when our average worldwide rate of increase was less than two percent. It is for this reason that I have been pressed and burdened to the extent that I can no longer bear it.

Therefore, in 1984, apparently through my own decision but actually under the Lord's leading, I returned to Taiwan. I felt that the situation could not continue in this way. I saw clearly that the truth among us cannot be changed and the life we have cannot be shaken, but the way we work must be changed in order to keep up with the need. It is true that no one can change the globe, because it was created by God. Man's standard of living on the globe, however, has been improving throughout the ages. One hundred years ago it took at least six months to sail from the West Coast of America to the East Coast of China, but today the methods of transportation have improved so much that one round-trip flight in an airplane takes only one day. This does not mean that the globe has changed or shrunk; rather, it means that methods of transportation have greatly improved, making travel more convenient.

Furthermore, the development of the television, telephone, and other telecommunication technologies has increased the spread of news. To prepare for the full-time training, nearly every day we have to make long-distance phone calls, and the calls are quite numerous. It is not like when I first went to America; back then I had to think carefully about what I would say before calling because I did not dare to waste a second. Now we have approximately seven hundred full-time trainees in the training center. They sleep, eat, and meet there without any problems. This is not a small matter. Just the matters of cooking three meals a day and arranging the sleeping quarters require our painstaking preparation, almost all of which has been accomplished entirely by fellowshipping on the telephone. This shows us that the globe has not changed, but the activities, the means of transportation, and the technologies of communication on the globe have been improved again and again. The messages we release here in Taipei can be heard simultaneously by telephone in numerous places in America.

This is why we must have a change in the system. In the recent ten years, I have been continuously and tirelessly exhorting the young co-workers in Taiwan, telling them that they must make a change. Almost every time they went to America I mentioned this matter to them. I told them that Taiwan has been reformed and is still improving in business, industry, education, and all other aspects, but in our church life we have made no reforms or improvements. Take the Gospel Bookroom as an example. The packaging of other bookstores has improved and changed for the better, but in our bookroom we have been doing things in the same way that we did thirty years ago without making a single change. I certainly never imagined that in the end I would have to return to Taiwan to lead all the churches to have a change.

I was very busy with my work in the United States and was bearing a heavy burden with no possibility of leaving, but in 1984 when I finished writing the footnotes to the last book of the Life-study of the New Testament, I told myself that I would return to Taiwan. The saints in America can all testify that when I returned this time it was not an easy thing. I put aside all my work in Anaheim and completely devoted my heart to Taiwan. My burden was to bring the Lord's recovery into a change of system here in Taiwan. We cannot change the Lord's recovery itself, nor can we change the truth and life, but surely we must change the rate of increase in the churches. I hope that in the matter of changing the system, Taiwan can become the "fellowship center" for the entire globe.

I have been speaking for the Lord for more than fifty years, but I never used the term *push* because I believed that it signified human effort. Now, however, I have changed, and I intend to use this word a lot. All the full-timers are my helpers to help me push the elders and the church in Taipei. The church in Taipei is like an old car which cannot be pulled or pushed, so I need these more than seven hundred full-timers to push together with me. In saying this word I might greatly offend the elders in Taipei, but my intention is good and proper. We have changed neither the truth nor the life. Rather, we still highly regard them as much as in the past. We are only changing our ways of working by correcting our errors and making improvements. If pushing does not work, then we will have to "stir" and "incite." Pushing is for something moveable, stirring is for something living, and inciting is for something weak. If the church in Taipei still would not move, I will have to ask these more than seven hundred full-timers to help me pick it up and carry it on our shoulders.

We are all one family. I am like the eldest in this family, and when I see the second, third, and even fourth generations among you being raised up, I am full of emotion in my heart. Especially among the elders, there are many who are only a little over thirty years old, of whom I feel very proud. However, if you do not move, cold water will be poured upon my pride. I am not blaming you. I am only blaming the fact that we have waited so long to change the system, because as early as 1974 I should have promoted this change. Even though it is now ten years too late, I believe the Lord will give me a period of time for us to have a success. My wife is very concerned about my physical health and hopes that this time while I am here, I can work less and rest more. But I am only concerned about one thing—changing the system. We absolutely must change the system.

THE FOCUS OF THE CHANGE IN SYSTEM— THE HOUSEHOLD

The focus of the change in system is the household. In the New Testament we see many sweet households, such as the household of Caesar (Phil. 4:22), the household of Cornelius (Acts 10:22-24), the household of Lydia, a seller of purple-dyed goods (16:13-15), and the household of the jailer whose name is unknown (vv. 29-34). There was also the household of Stephanas (1 Cor. 1:16) and the household of Crispus (Acts 18:8). In addition, there were houses in which the meetings were held, such as Aquila and Prisca's house (Rom. 16:3-5; 1 Cor. 16:19), the house of Nymphas (Col. 4:15), and the house of Philemon (Philem. 1-2). These examples clearly show us that the unit of God's salvation and service is the household.

Even in the Old Testament, in the two great types of salvation, the household was the unit of salvation. The first was the type of the flood in which the eight members of the house of Noah entered into the ark and were thus saved from God's judgment on the world (Gen. 7:1; Heb. 11:7; 2 Pet. 2:5). The second was the type of the Passover in which each Israelite household took a lamb, killed it, put the blood on the doorposts and the lintel of the house, and ate the flesh of the lamb. It was not a lamb for each person but for each household as a unit (Exo. 12:3-8). In the past we have ignored these clear truths of the Bible; we were influenced by Christianity and were distracted and carried away.

From the beginning of the Lord's recovery in China, Brother Nee pointed out that the church needs to be built up with the household as a unit. I received this matter from him and brought the practice to Taiwan. In addition, I introduced the practice of the "groups." However, in 1984 when I returned to Taiwan, these two practices were almost non-existent. We were under the influence of the nations and were following their customs (2 Kings 17:33) to walk in the way of the denominations in Christianity by copying their practice of big meetings in which one man speaks while all the rest listen. This practice brings forth the "clergy" and the "laity," which prevents not every saint from functioning. Seeing this, I want to bring out a specific way for our practice at this crucial time.

DEFINITE STEPS NEEDED FOR PRACTICING THE CHANGE OF SYSTEM

Having an Average of One Full-time Serving One Out of Every Twenty Saints

Out of every twenty saints meeting in the Lord's recovery there should be one full-time serving one. Although I cannot say that this is a revelation from the Lord, I feel very clear inwardly that this is an excellent way. I also trumpeted this call very clearly in the United States, hoping that all the more than six hundred churches on the six continents would be able to do this. This is the first principle for carrying out our change of system: that one out of twenty of the saints would be full-time.

Some news has come in from two local churches. One locality which has one hundred eighty in the meetings is willing to produce nine full-timers, and the other locality which has eighty in the meetings will produce four full-timers. Now the church in Taipei, which has four thousand people regularly attending the meetings, has produced two hundred full-timers. This altogether corresponds to the principle of one out of twenty. I am very happy about this.

Having an Average of One Out of Every Four Saints Go Out Door-knocking

The second principle is that out of every four saints there should be one who goes out door-knocking. This does not refer to the door-knocking which is to be carried out by the full-timers; rather, this means that in the seven days of one week, one out of every four saints should set aside two hours to go out door-knocking. This does not require you to do a lot;

you need to go only once a week. However, you must be persistent in this and do it every week. Unless you or a family member is ill and needs to rest or be cared for, you all should keep this principle and practice going out door-knocking for two hours every week.

Luke 9 says that when the Lord was calling people to follow Him, someone said to Him, "Lord, permit me to go first and bury my father." The Lord said, "Let the dead bury their own dead, but you go and announce the kingdom of God everywhere." Another one said, "I will follow you, Lord; but first permit me to say farewell to those in my house." The Lord said, "No one who puts his hand on the plow and looks behind is fit for the kingdom of God" (vv. 59-62). According to this portion of the Word, we can also say that no matter what happens in our homes, we should always adhere to the principle of spending two hours a week to go out door-knocking. There are no excuses; nothing is so important that it can keep us from going out. No matter how busy we are, we must go out for two hours a week. There are fifty-two weeks a year, and as long as we are able to go, then we should practice this principle every week without fail.

I am speaking this word not to the full-timers but to all the saints. We all have a desire to serve the Lord because we love Him. Now the Lord wants us to set apart two hours a week for Him, so how can we say that He is asking too much? There are one hundred sixty-eight hours in a week, and two hours is only about one percent. If we really love Him, how can we refuse? If we cannot do even this much, how can we be excused? Regardless of who you are or how busy you are, you should give the Lord two hours every week to do nothing else but go out door-knocking.

A WAY OF RECEIVING THE BLESSING

Now I have no desire to speak any doctrines. I just want to promote the new way for the Lord's recovery. The first point of the new way is that of the saints who regularly meet, one in twenty should be a full-timer, and the second point is that one in four should go out door-knocking for two hours every week.

If a local church would be willing to practice these two principles, it will certainly be greatly blessed.

The full-timers should also go out door-knocking from Monday through Saturday for at least two or three hours a day. If a full-time serving one would be willing to do this, I believe that every week he would gain and baptize at least one person. In this way he would gain about fifty people in a year. At this rate the church in Taipei with its two hundred full-timers would gain ten thousand people in one year.

I hope that we all would be able to hear and receive this word. The two hundred full-timers supported by four thousand people should spend every day studying the truth, serving the church, and caring for the saints. In addition, they should set aside two or three hours every day to go out door-knocking, and each of these two hundred should be able to gain about fifty people a year. This means that these two hundred would bring in ten thousand people through door-knocking. This truly is a profitable matter.

This is the conclusion we drew from our practical research. If the Lord allows it, the Chinese Recovery Version of the New Testament will be finished next year, and then I will go to every continent to speak the same thing. On the one hand, I hate that I am so old now that I am not qualified to be a soldier, and on the other hand, I am certainly bearing too many burdens. Otherwise, I would definitely go out door-knocking every day.

A NEW AND EFFECTIVE WAY

We must be clear, however, that when the church is about to move ahead, we cannot avoid having some who will blow cold wind or pour cold water on us because they think that it is of no use to gain new ones. They say that when you have many births, the number of deaths increases also. Therefore, they believe it is better to give birth to just a few and save the trouble. Actually, even if we take away the percentage of those who are lost, dragging, or unreliable, we will still be able to gain some reliable and remaining fruit as our increase, our multiplication.

More than sixty years ago Brother Nee and I often told the

saints that we should double our number every year. After coming to Taiwan, I said the same thing—that we should double our number every year—whenever I mentioned the matter of increase. By 1984 when I returned to fellowship about the new way and to practice the change of system, I mentioned this matter again. This time it was in a public stadium, and you all stood up and responded to my fellowship, promising to bring one person to salvation every year and saying that the church membership would double. Today, two years later, what is the result? You have not saved many because you have not had an effective way. You have expended much time and energy, but your efforts have been wasted. This time I would like to fellowship with you a specific way for our practice. If you are willing to do things in this way, we will definitely be able to double our numbers in one year. Furthermore, it will be with remaining, reliable fruit. If this is the case, it will take only four years for four thousand to increase to sixty-four thousand. How could we not be excited about this?

To use a common saying, if we are not willing to make this kind of "business deal," we are really foolish. According to the Lord's word, if we reject this kind of fellowship, when we meet the Lord, we will not be able to give an account before Him (Matt. 25:14-30). We are accountable not to men but to the Lord. This is not a loose or careless word. This is the Lord's word which will be fulfilled at His judgment seat (2 Cor. 5:10; Rom. 14:10). Today among us the truth is clear and rich, and the leading of the Holy Spirit is definite and trustworthy. We certainly must not be slow to respond or hesitate to make a move. An increase at the rate of doubling the number every year is something without precedent in the history of Christianity. This matter alone is worthwhile for us to give our whole strength and expend our entire being.

I suggested to all the elders in Taipei that they should pass on this burden to all the saints and ask every one of them to write a consecration slip at the table meeting on the Lord's Day. Whoever has a heart to love the Lord should consecrate themselves especially to go out door-knocking every week for two hours. Beginning next week I will train these consecrated ones, stir up the fire of their love, give them a definite way to practice, and teach them how to go out door-knocking.

THE CHURCHES' COORDINATION CONCERNING THE NEW WAY

In the first term of the Full-time Training, there were seven hundred attendants. According to my observation, the trainees have already learned the first step of how to knock on doors and lead people to believe and be baptized. But after these people are saved, there are three more steps we need to get into in a deeper way. The second step is that we must go to people's homes after they have been baptized to continue meeting with them. We must have meetings in their homes. The third step is that after we have set up a meeting in their homes, we must teach them the truth and help them to grow in life. This is not very easy to do. The fourth step is that while we are teaching people the truth and helping them to grow in life, we must help them to have the full knowledge concerning the church and to live in the practical church life.

In this term of training we have already baptized 4,800 people. Of these people, 2,600 are reliable, and we have established 1,000 home meetings. After a month, when the training is over, how will the church in Taipei care for these 2,600 people and these 1,000 home meetings? This is a pressing problem for us to resolve. For this, the church in Taipei must raise up at least 1,000 people who will go out to visit these new ones and care for them in the home meetings. This is a matter which cannot be delayed, and I hope that the elders will pick up a great burden and pray much for this and that the saints will also receive this fellowship.

There is one point about which we must be clear. Although you have turned in your consecration slips expressing a desire to go out door-knocking for two hours every week, it still must be approved by the elders. If some of you are not chosen, you should not be disappointed. You can still continue to pray and contribute your money and strength to support and supply this move. As to who should go out door-knocking every week and who should stay home to support by praying and making monetary contributions, this matter will be decided by the elders. We will be responsible for training the consecrated ones. Later they will all come to the training center to be blended together and to coordinate together for visiting and caring for new ones or for continuing to go out door-knocking in order to gain more people. This is a definite and practical way which I hope you will carry out steadfastly.

I believe that none of the saints who love the Lord and are for His recovery would disagree, nor should any disagree, with this fellowship. We have neither changed the truth nor negated the life. Rather, we have just had a new breakthrough with regard to the way of preaching the gospel, releasing the truth, and leading others to follow the Lord and come into the church life. We should make progress in this matter. In the world today, no matter what field you are in, the practical methods are constantly being reformed and improved. This is true even in the field of education. Therefore, we definitely must not cling to the old ways. Because Taiwan keeps updating its concepts, every aspect of society is able to prosper. I hope that we also would be able to make changes and be renewed in order that the numbers in the churches could grow and increase.

In order to practice this new way, we must be in one accord. The way has been clearly set forth before our eyes; if we continue to loosely express our opinions at will, we will make a mess of the whole situation. Changing the system is necessary, and our way of practice is excellent. All that is needed is for us to carry it out in one accord. The saints who meet regularly must produce one full-timer for every twenty saints to go out door-knocking every day. They must also produce one door-knocker for every four saints to go out door-knocking for two hours every week without fail. The elders should encourage and stir up the saints to consecrate themselves. Then the saints should receive training, be put into groups, and go out to knock on doors and care for others. If the churches cooperate in this way, I believe that the increase in the churches will ensure for us a great future.

PRACTICING THE NEW WAY
IN THE LIGHT OF THE RECOVERY

Scripture Reading: Matt. 28:18-20; Acts 2:46; 5:42; 1 Tim. 2:4; Eph. 3:8-11

CHRISTIANITY MISSING GOD'S ECONOMY

Concerning God's divine economy, we must mention some history. It has now been sixty-four years since the early part of this century when the Lord raised up His recovery in the Far East. During this time the Lord has shown us many divine revelations. Especially in the last twenty-three years, since the Lord brought His recovery to the West, we have published the greatest number of books among us, even double the number we had published in the first forty-one years. All together about three thousand messages have been put out. The content of these messages is nothing other than the revelation of the Bible concerning the Triune God in His Divine Trinity—Father, Son, and Spirit—working Himself into all the believers of Christ. This is the main subject of the Bible, but for the most part it is not taught in Christianity; instead, Christianity has ignored it, even missed it.

God's economy is that the Triune God in His Divine Trinity—Father, Son, and Spirit—is working Himself into those who have believed into Christ that they may be regenerated, sanctified, transformed, and even completely conformed, within and without, to the image not of the only begotten Son but of the firstborn Son of God (Rom. 8:29). The only begotten Son of God had only divinity without humanity. He was only God but not man. The firstborn Son of God, however, has both divinity and humanity. He is not only the complete God but also the perfect Man. This is a marvelous matter. In His divine economy the Triune God intends to work Himself into us, beginning with our regeneration and continuing with our sanctification, transformation, and conformation until we have been conformed to the same image as Christ, the firstborn Son of God, in both divinity and humanity (2 Cor. 3:18; 1 John 3:2).

In this way Christ becomes the firstborn Son of God, and we become the many sons of God. In the universe God has obtained a group of sons out of His old creation through His work of the new creation. These sons are the many brothers of His firstborn Son and the many members of the Body of Christ (Rom. 12:5). These many members and Christ constitute the one new man (Eph. 2:15). God has His many sons, and Christ has His many members. These many sons of God constitute His house for His kingdom, and these many members of Christ constitute His Body as the corporate expression of the Triune God, the totality and the ultimate consummation and manifestation of which is the New Jerusalem. The church today is the miniature of the New Jerusalem.

Over the past twenty-three years we have put out messages concerning God's economy again and again. Regrettably, Christianity, for the most part, neither knows nor inquires about this economy of God. In other words, nearly all of Christianity has become a religion which at most preaches to sinners in a shallow way about the name of Jesus and His gospel in the Bible and helps them to be saved by repenting and believing in the Lord Jesus. Most people do not even know that to be regenerated is to receive the life of God as their life apart from and in addition to man's own life. In their view, regeneration is similar to what the Chinese call "putting away the old and turning over a new leaf," that is, everything of yesterday is over and dead, while everything of today has a fresh beginning.

Thus, nearly all of Christianity has no understanding of and is entirely lacking in such matters as God's economy, Christ as the mystery of God, the church as the mystery of Christ, and Christ and the church as the great mystery. In 1 Timothy 3:9 Paul tells the saints who are deacons that they must hold "the mystery of the faith in a pure conscience." In verse 15 he goes on to say that the church is the house of the living God, the pillar and base of the truth. Today if we were to ask Christianity's professors of theology, pastors, or famous evangelists what "the mystery of the faith" is or what "truth" is, most of them would answer that a mystery is a mystery, so man certainly cannot understand it. Concerning truth, they would say that it simply means "doctrine."

Actually, the truth in 1 Timothy 3:15 refers to the reality of the universe. First, the reality of the universe is the Triune God. Originally, everything in the universe was entirely vanity because all things would pass away. Nothing is real or reliable; neither the heavens nor the earth is reliable. The only reality in the universe is the Triune God Himself. This Triune God has a heart's desire which is to work Himself into His chosen people by passing through some processes. This is why the Lord Jesus came and announced that He is the reality (John 14:6). This means that as the embodiment of the Triune God, He is the reality of the universe. Later, the Holy Spirit came as the Spirit of reality, the Spirit of truth, not to teach people the biblical truths but to be the reality of the Triune God, dispensing Him into people as reality.

Furthermore, the word of God is also reality because the word of God brings God, Christ, and the Holy Spirit into us. For this reason, the Lord said that His words are spirit and life (6:63). Today when we contact the Bible, we are contacting neither a book of theology nor a book of doctrines. Rather, we are receiving the God and Christ of reality; that is, we are receiving spirit and life imparted to us through the holy Word.

The church is the pillar and base of this reality. The church upholds neither doctrines nor theology but reality. Once there was a student at a Christian seminary who testified that in the first year of his theological studies the students believed that God existed, in the second year they doubted His existence, in the third year they began to deny Him, and by the fourth year they utterly denied Him and did not believe that He was real. Another student of theology told me that attending seminary was terrible and that in the end the students were just left with an "ism" or an "ology." They studied "tritheism" and "Christology," but in the end they had neither God nor Christ, just an "ism" and an "ology."

I thoroughly understand Christianity, having contacted it for so many years in both the East and the West. I can even say that I have thoroughly studied Western Christianity. I have seen it all clearly. The majority of those in Christianity do not have the proper concept of the truth, and they have completely ignored God's economy. When I went to the West with my full preaching of God's truth, some immediately responded with more than twenty publications slandering me for preaching the Eastern philosophy of pantheism. I have contacted some among them who have much theological knowledge. Although they know that the Bible speaks about God's economy, they have not entered into that economy. On the contrary, they have remained stuck in their familiar theology. What Christianity has given the world today are things such as the Christmas tree and Easter eggs. I once met a pious Christian in America who was unable to give up his Christmas tree because his wife and children liked it. This is the impression given by Christianity.

TEACHING GOD'S ECONOMY IN THE HOME MEETINGS

Today we must pay attention to the truth when we go out door-knocking. After bringing people to be saved and baptized, we must set up meetings in their homes for the purpose of teaching them the truth and helping them to grow in life. In Matthew 28:19-20a the Lord Jesus charged the disciples, saying, "Go therefore and disciple all the nations, baptizing them into the name of the Father and of the Son and of the Holy Spirit, teaching them to observe all that I have commanded you." After telling the disciples to baptize people into the name of the Father, the Son, and the Holy Spirit, the Lord Jesus charged them to teach people not about celebrating Christmas and Easter but about observing the truths which He had commanded them.

In the four Gospels the Lord Jesus spoke three long messages. In the first message, in Matthew 5—7, He spoke about the constitution of the kingdom; in the second message, in

Matthew 13, He used seven parables to unveil the mysteries of the kingdom; and in the third message, in John 14—16, He spoke about the mystery of the Triune God. At that time, these were the things which the Lord commanded the disciples to teach to the believers. However, up to this day, in which so-called church are these messages preached? The pastors preach mostly things such as God being love and the Lord letting the little children come to Him to be blessed by Him (Matt. 19:13-15). These kinds of messages are entirely outside of the central lane of the Lord's teachings.

In our change of system today, when we practice the new way of going out door-knocking to bring people to be saved and baptized into the Triune God, we must follow up by teaching them the divine truths. Instead of bringing them to the meeting hall, however, we should go to their homes and teach them. Acts tells us that the disciples practiced according to the Lord's command. After the three thousand were saved on the day of Pentecost, they broke bread from house to house (2:46). Later, another five thousand were saved, and they did the same thing. Furthermore, Acts tells us that the apostles went from house to house preaching the gospel and teaching people (5:42). They did not teach the shallow doctrines of today's Christianity. Instead, they taught about God's New Testament economy concerning Christ and the church as revealed in the entire New Testament. They did not build meeting halls or worship halls for gathering people to be taught. Instead, they went from house to house teaching people. This was the persistent and prevailing practice in the early churches (cf. Rom. 16:5; 1 Cor. 16:19; Col. 4:15; Philem. 2). Today, we also must return to the original practices of going to the new believers' homes to establish meetings and teach them the truths, especially those in Matthew 5—7 and 13 and in John 14—16.

Since we have to teach people, we ourselves must first know the truth. The New Testament Recovery Version includes a chart of the seventy weeks with the coming of Christ and the rapture of the saints. After reading the chart, many people still find it hard to understand. Actually, if we want to understand the mystery of God's economy, we must first

understand Matthew 5—7, Matthew 13, and John 14—16. In the
Recovery Version of the New Testament these chapters have
footnotes that are very clear, and we must study them deeply
in order to help others understand what God's economy is.
This is the burden in the depths of my inner being. Therefore,
when we go to lead the home meetings, we should teach God's
economy.

First Timothy 2:4 says that God desires all men to be
saved and to come to the full knowledge of the truth. Three
months have already passed in this term of the training, and
the trainees have gone out door-knocking and have already
baptized five thousand people. We praise the Lord for this,
but we can offer only partial praise because God wants all
men not only to be saved but also to come to the full knowledge of the truth. In Greek this phrase is *come to the full
knowledge,* so it is not just a small amount of knowledge. God
wants all men to be saved, and He wants them also to come to
the full knowledge of the truth. This is not an easy or light
matter.

Therefore, as we are changing the system to practice the
new way, there are four definite steps in our going out door-
knocking from house to house: first, leading people to believe
and be baptized; second, feeding and taking care of them by
setting up meetings in their homes; third, teaching them the
truth in their homes and at the same time ministering life to
them; and fourth, bringing them into the full knowledge of
the church and into the practical church life.

THE REAL GOSPEL—CONCERNING THE ECONOMY
OF THE MYSTERY OF GOD

In Ephesians 3:8-11 Paul said that although he was not a
great apostle but was less than the least of all saints, he had
received mercy and grace to announce to people the "unsearchable riches of Christ as the gospel and to enlighten all that
they may see what the economy of the mystery is, which
throughout the ages had been hidden in God, who created all
things, in order that now to the rulers and the authorities in
the heavenlies the multifarious wisdom of God might be made
known through the church." Thus, the real gospel is not about

heaven and hell, sin and forgiveness, perdition and eternal life, or suffering and blessing; the real gospel is about the mystery of God's economy.

In God there is a mystery which is His economy. In His economy the Triune God became the all-inclusive Spirit by passing through various processes so that, as such a Spirit, He can enter into men with His redemption, all-inclusive death on the cross, resurrection, ascension, divinity, and humanity. When the all-inclusive Spirit as the consummation of the Triune God is received into men, He first regenerates them. Then He brings them through the work of sanctification and transformation until they are conformed to the image of the firstborn Son of God to be the many sons of God and the many brothers of Christ, constituting the house of God and the Body of Christ for the expression of Christ. When Satan and his followers see this house, this Body, which is the church, they will know the multifarious wisdom of God. This is the mystery of God's economy.

Paul's commission was to enlighten all that they may see this mystery. Our God does not just want people to know this mystery; He especially wants to show this to Satan. It is as if He wants to boast to Satan, saying, "Satan, you are very clever and crooked like a serpent. You get everything you want by hook or by crook. Nevertheless, you have only cleverness. I have wisdom. Two thousand years ago you began to employ your craftiness and to show off your cleverness, and you have been doing so until now. But in the end whatever you have done will have been all for the expression of My wisdom." This accomplishment of God is according to the plan, the purpose, which He made in eternity past. This is His economy.

SPENDING TIME TO GET INTO
AND TEACH THE TRUTHS OF THE RECOVERY

In this period when nearly all of Christianity has been ignoring His economy, God needs a further recovery in order to accomplish all that He has revealed, promised, and prophesied in the Bible. Through Brother Nee, this recovery was brought in among us. The Lord's recovery is different from Christianity. Even our going out door-knocking to preach the gospel is different from what Christianity is doing. When we go out door-knocking, we first preach using *The Mystery of Human Life* to show people that man was created with three parts: spirit, soul, and body. This is to let people know that God created man in this way for the purpose of having man as His vessel to contain Him, so that He could enter into man, and in the end man could express Him. Many who have been Christians for years still may not be clear about this truth, but today when we go out door-knocking, the first thing we give people is this truth, and when they hear it, they are saved. This kind of gospel preaching is revolutionary and of the recovery.

Some have asked why the Recovery Version of the New Testament has the word *Recovery* in its title and what it is that needs to be recovered. Recovery is to recover the truths lost by Christianity, the truths which the worldly theology cannot understand, and the truths which most theology professors have never seen and are not willing to touch, such as God's economy and His dispensing. The entire New Testament begins with a genealogy (Matt. 1:1-17). Formerly, not many people understood this genealogy, but today if anyone reads the Recovery Version of the New Testament, he only needs to read the footnotes for about ten minutes in order to be able to understand its deep significance. Thus, what we call the recovery is a recovery of the divine truths in the Bible.

The full-time training established by the church is not a training in methods; rather, it is a training to get the saints into the truth. The truth produces life. If the trainees study the truth every day according to their schedule, in the end they will spontaneously be nourished due to their knowledge of the truth. After they have been built up in this way, if they go out door-knocking, they will bring people to be saved by the recovery truths, and these new ones will be solid. Then, the trainees will set up meetings in the homes of these new believers and teach them more of the recovery truths, such as God's economy, His dispensing, His eternal plan, and the processes He went through to accomplish His economy. Thus, the new ones will be established in the truth.

In the past, we were accustomed to big meetings with one person speaking and everyone else listening. However, after all that speaking and listening, some who have been meeting with us for thirty or forty years have not even graduated from spiritual elementary school. They are not even clear about how they themselves were saved. This is because they have never studied the truth thoroughly. Now we have put out the *Truth Lessons,* but the sad thing is that we lack teachers. I am afraid we will be like the blind leading the blind, and everyone will fall into a pit. Therefore, the teachers must first study and get into the truth before they can teach the saints.

In the same way, since we all have a heart to go out door-knocking and to care for people, we must spend time to get into the truth. The training gives us a way to get into the truth. How much we gain, though, depends upon the price we pay. Nevertheless, it is much easier for us to get into the truth today than it was fifty years ago. Fifty years ago, if we wanted to study the genealogy in Matthew, it was hard to find a book explaining it. If we wanted to study the parables in Matthew 13, it was hard to find a proper reference book. Once I found a book which said that the leaven in the meal is a positive thing, referring to the gospel and truth in Christianity which are able to influence all of society. When I first read this, I felt it was very good, but later my eyes were opened to know that it was absolutely not in accord with the truth. Today in the Lord's recovery the truth is clear, and there are many books to which we can refer and which will help us get into the truth. However, it is entirely up to us to spend the time to study them.

When doing a certain thing, each person will do it differently, and the results will be related to the person doing it. Take door-knocking as an example: the president, a bank manager, a university professor, and a street sweeper could all go door-knocking, but each would have a different "flavor." This is not a matter of how loud a person's voice is or how refined his tone is, but a matter of what kind of person he is. When we go door-knocking today, and a person answers the door, if we know the truth, we will be full of the flavor of the truth. However, if we do not know the truth, what we speak

will be merely commonplace. Therefore, we must equip ourselves with the truth and "truthize" ourselves. Then we
should take the truth with which we have been "truthized" to
"truthize" others until all Taiwan has been "truthized." Some
people may think that this standard is too high. I admit that it
is high. The education system in Taiwan, however, has
improved and industry and business are being revolutionized
at an incredible rate, so I believe that this standard is attainable. When I was still young, the word *technology* was not in
the Chinese language, but now this word is used by everyone.
In the Lord's recovery, we are not doing the work of Christianity or preaching the gospel that they preach. Rather, we
are preaching the unsearchable riches of Christ as the gospel
just as Paul did (Eph. 3:8-11). Acts 5:42 says, "Announcing
the gospel of Jesus as the Christ." This is the high gospel.
Therefore, we must equip ourselves by spending time to study
the truth. We should not take the easy way.

THE NEW WAY REVEALED BY GOD— DELIVERING THE GOSPEL AND THE TRUTH TO PEOPLES' HOMES

Whatever God does is always wise, and whatever man
thinks is always foolish. In the Bible we cannot find the phrase
come and hear the gospel. There is not such a thought in the
Bible. The biblical concept is not one of inviting people to come
but of telling us to go. Consider this: if the Lord Jesus had
just sat in the heavens on the throne and sent the angels to
invite people up to heaven to hear the gospel, no one would
have been able to get there. Instead, our Lord came personally
to bring the gospel to people. John 4 says that one day when
He was going from Judea into Galilee, He had to pass through
Samaria, but He purposely got off the main road and detoured
to Sychar to bring the gospel to a specific place—the well of
Jacob, which was near Sychar. This means He foreknew that
the immoral woman would go there at noon to draw water.
In the ancient times in the area around Judea, women usually
went out to draw water in the evening as the sun was setting,
and they would also go out in groups. However, because this
woman was immoral, no one would have anything to do with

her. As a result, she would not go out in the evenings lest people point at her and gossip about her. Therefore, she went out under the hot sun of midday to draw water when no one else was around. No one else knew, but the Lord Jesus knew and waited for her beside the well. You can see to what lengths the Lord Jesus went so that He could deliver the gospel!

Today the Mormons and the Jehovah's Witnesses go out door-knocking, and even some in Christianity who love the Lord also go out door-knocking with gospel tracts. Our door-knocking, however, is different from theirs because we learn from the Lord. The Lord Jesus was the leading One in this matter. He went to Samaria, which was an improper place of mixture, not to contact a high-class person but to contact a low-class woman who had had five husbands and was now living with one who was not her husband. Moreover, the Lord went to Jericho, an accursed city, to deliver the gospel not to the house of a gentleman but to the house of a tax collector who was also a cheater and extortionist (Luke 19:1-10). Therefore, when we send out invitations asking people to come and hear the gospel, strictly speaking, we are not acting according to the biblical principle. God's way is to deliver the gospel to people, but often our way is to invite people to come. When people come at our invitation, they are doing us a favor, so we have to give them thanks. When we go door-knocking, apparently we are bothering people, but in the end they will thank us.

This is a busy world; every family and every person is busy. Nevertheless, every evening and holiday many people are just busy watching television or reading the newspaper to fill up their time of boredom. If we go out door-knocking and visit them at these times, they will certainly be interested and welcome us in to speak with them. They are watching and reading the earthly things, but we are speaking to them the heavenly things. I believe they certainly will be attracted. There is a full-time trainee, a brother, who has gained one hundred seventeen through door-knocking. In eternity, I believe that many will thank him, saying, "How good it is that you came to my door one day and brought me the gospel! I really thank you." When we look back on our own salvation, do we not thank those who brought us to the Lord? Even in the New Jerusalem, we will still thank them. I believe that many people will say to those who went out door-knocking, "If it were not for your coming to visit me every week for three months, I would never have been saved or have been able to participate in the new heaven and the new earth. I really thank you."

The practice of going out door-knocking is God's wise ordination, and it is the new way which is welcomed by people. This is very different from inviting people to hear the gospel. In principle, most people do not like to accept this kind of invitation, but they welcome our visiting them by door-knocking. We, however, must equip ourselves to be rich in the truth and full grown, matured in life. Especially when we go out door-knocking, we can no longer be children or speak like little children. As soon as we open our mouths, people will be able to smell the aroma of what kind of person we are. If someone is a college student, once he opens his mouth, it will be a college student's aroma. If someone is an elementary school student, when he opens his mouth, it will be the aroma of a child in elementary school. Opening our mouth and speaking will immediately reveal or expose how much cargo we possess inwardly. Therefore, we must equip ourselves. At the same time we must pray to allow the Lord to fill us inwardly until our entire being is filled with the Lord and overflowing with the Spirit. Then, regardless of whether we go out door-knocking or attend a home meeting, it will not be simply we who go, but the Lord and the Spirit will go with us. Then we will be different.

NEEDING TO DEAL WITH PRIDE AND OPINION
FOR THE PRACTICE OF THE NEW WAY

In 1984 when I received the burden to begin changing the system, I had the assurance inwardly because I knew what the Lord wanted. But I also foresaw that the brothers and sisters would have differing opinions, because changing the system would change the way we do things. Whenever there is a change in the way we do things, even if it is changing from an old way to a new way by getting rid of inappropriate things and building up the proper things, there will always be some who disagree. For example, I was accustomed to wearing a certain pair of slippers, but one day my wife noticed that these slippers were old and unbecoming, so she bought a new pair of slippers. Yet I still loved my old slippers because they matched my tastes and my habits. Even though the new slippers were good, I was not used to them. In the end my wife still "changed the system" by throwing away the old slippers and having me wear the new slippers. Although I had a different opinion, I got used to them in three to five days. In the same way, when we change the system and take the new way, some people will have a different opinion because they are not accustomed to it. I believe, however, that in the end no one will have a different opinion, because the new way is the God-ordained way.

I have never cared about or investigated differing opinions. Two weeks ago I received a telephone call from a certain brother who asked me what he should do. In his locality the young people wanted to take the new way, but the older ones would not agree. As a result, the young ones said some things they should not have said, and now there might be a division. I told him not to worry because the young people in the church life are like the young children in a family who are sometimes naughty and break a window. All you have to do is spend some money to have it fixed; you do not have to fight with them. The church is like a family, so we can let the young ones "play" and do not need to worry that a problem may arise.

My point is this: Today after the full-time trainees finish the training, they may be very learned and think highly of themselves because they have graduated from the university and have also learned how to go door-knocking and how to get a person to believe and be baptized in fifteen minutes. Therefore, when they go back to their local churches, they will be very proud and happy. This is wrong and improper. Young people should not be proud, but on the other hand, I also hope that the older saints would not criticize these young ones too much. The older saints have their good points. Take the church in Taipei as an example. Our older saints are very faithful. Sometimes a storm comes up, but they are calm and unmoved. When another storm comes up, they simply ignore it. The reason the church in Taipei has survived until today is entirely because these ones are here. Although I have somewhat criticized the church in Taipei in the matter of the increase, I would still say that the most stable church in the world today is the church in Taipei. The saints here are not only clear concerning the truth and proper in their way, but also they are truly walking practically in the truth and standing on the ground of oneness. However, because we are still human, sometimes when we see these young people, who have been saved for only five or six years, murmuring and criticizing us, it is hard for us not to be angry. Please do not rebuke them immediately. On the contrary, you should try to find a time to exhort them patiently.

In the church, regardless of whether you are old or young, you all need to bear and help one another instead of making demands on or criticizing each other. The young trainees should not overemphasize the fact that they are taking the new way and have gained so many people through door-knocking. The older ones should not shake their heads, thinking that these trainees, who have just knocked on a few doors and gained a few people who may or may not be reliable, simply cannot compare with themselves who are so stable and steadfast in the church for so many years. Some localities have divided into parties over this matter of promoting the new way but because we know there cannot be division in the church, we still meet in one place while we sit in our parties on different sides. This is not pleasing to God, and I hope none of you would be proud or consider yourself to be stronger than others.

The older saints should get credit for their hard work, if not for their achievement, in establishing and maintaining the testimony of the church. In this respect, the young people must honor and appreciate the older ones. The younger ones must be humble before the elderly fathers. They should be aggressive in the matter of door-knocking, not in the way they deal with the older saints. Some of the older saints cannot get used to the new way, so the younger ones should not boast in front of them. Instead, they should be quiet and not proud. Over a long period of time, the older ones will trust you and let you do as you see fit. Do not think of pushing them to follow you; their function is to be guardians of the church. You should just boldly go out door-knocking. Later, when you have brought people to salvation and have slowly brought some into the church life, the older saints will see this, and even if in the past they blew cold wind and poured cold water on you, they will be really happy in their hearts. They are only worried that you will not bear remaining fruit. Their hearts are good, so you must still bring your new ones to them for confirmation.

Furthermore, the young people must learn not to have any opinions. When I was young in the denominations and later when I came into the Lord's recovery, I never had any opinions with respect to those older than I. Today in the Lord's recovery, the saints in every local church all love the Lord and are for the Lord's recovery, so we do not need to have opinions. Instead, we should coordinate together, striving to keep the oneness of the Spirit. In this term of the training five thousand people have been saved through door-knocking, and one thousand home meetings have been established. By the end of the training, even more people will have been saved and even more home meetings will have been established. In time the older saints will feel comforted and will appreciate the new way, admitting that it is wonderful. This will keep the oneness of the church and will also keep the church in the oneness of the Spirit without any opinions.

I hope that all of us would be able to receive this balancing word. The church needs the older saints and the younger saints, just as a country needs the older people for maintaining it and the younger people for fighting. But people are very strange. When they are in the army, they always say the army is good and important, but when they are discharged, they say that the army is not good. When a person is doing something personally, he or she says that it is good. Teachers say teaching is good, and businessmen say doing business is good. When they are no longer occupying that particular position or doing that particular job, they say that it is not good. These things are difficult to avoid, so we should not be bothered by them.

THE CONTROLLING VISION
FOR PRACTICING THE NEW WAY

We must clearly recognize that the burden and commission which we have received from the Lord are not just to go out door-knocking and to lead people to salvation. Rather, we must gain a group of new ones who will be for God's economy. Today the world population is about 4.6 billion, and the number of Christians and Catholics added together still does not equal one-third of the entire world population. All the rest of the people are non-Christians. Moreover, the Christian group in Taiwan with the greatest number of people is the Presbyterian Church, and they have only a little more than 100,000 believers. The local churches are the next largest with 40,000 or 50,000. The third is the True Jesus Church with 20,000 or 30,000. The total added together does not even equal 200,000, as all the rest of the Christian groups have just a few scattered members. Taiwan is such a modern place, yet it has so few Christians. Therefore, when we go out door-knocking, our principal target is still non-Christians. If we do knock on the door of a Catholic or a Christian, we should not try to change them, nor should we reject them. We should just give them *The Mystery of Human Life*. If they would not receive it, we should politely go away. We must always remember that in the entire world there are more than 3 billion unbelievers who are the main target of our door-knocking. We must let Christianity go its own way. We will gain new ones for the Lord's recovery.

This is why we need to be trained. This training is not to train us in methods or techniques but to train us in the truth, that we all could be filled with the truth. Then when we go out door-knocking we would not just gain some people but would help them to know the truth. I have said before that if we take four thousand as the basic number for Taipei and practice according to what we have fellowshipped, then in four years we should be able to gain 2.7 million people. Then Taipei would really be evangelized. I do know that among those whom we gain, probably only a small number will be reliable and stable. Nevertheless, even those unreliable Christians who do not come to meetings are beneficial to us.

In the place where I am staying there are several potted plants. One day I saw an orchid on my coffee table that had roots, branches, and leaves, but only one flower. I realized that any particular thing needs many outward items to support and cultivate its inward substance. In the same way, if 2.7 million people are baptized, then most of them are "roots," "branches," and "leaves," but very few "outshine" others to be the "flower." Therefore, we should not be worried if the new ones are unreliable or if perhaps there are some false ones among them; sometimes false Christians are beneficial to us. Even at the time of the apostle Paul there were some unreliable ones in the church. Paul was one who received the highest revelation and who led the Corinthians to salvation, yet the Corinthians turned around and said that he had been crafty and taken them by guile for the purpose of getting their money (cf. 2 Cor. 12:16). I believe that God has a record of this, so there is no need to worry. We just need to allow those predestined to salvation to be saved and let those who would oppose do so. Our goal is that all the people in Taipei would be saved.

In 1949 I began the work in Taipei, and the whole meeting hall was full of people on the first day. Because every one of them had come with a different purpose, I told them, "You go to a certain kind of restaurant to eat a certain kind of food. We do not have a Shantung restaurant, so if some of you want to eat steamed bread, you have come to the wrong place." I expected that the numbers on the next Lord's Day would certainly be smaller and that those who came would want to eat our food, so I asked the business office to prepare cards for signing up. As expected, less than half showed up; most of the others never came again. I just worked with those who came back, and it brought in the Lord's great blessing.

In this age the Lord has certainly revealed all the visions in the New Testament to us, enabling us to clearly see God's economy. Now we should be faithful to go out door-knocking to gain some for this economy and to feed the new ones for this economy by teaching them the truth. On the other hand, we ourselves must live in this economy. In this way, we will have such a group of people under the light of the truth who are being taught, cultivated, and supplied and who in their daily lives live Christ, express Him, and have become one spirit with Him, living in the spirit and walking by the spirit. This is what the Lord wants to obtain today. When the Lord returns, these ones will be the bride for Him to gain and the firstfruits who are raptured first. It is such a group of people who can cause the Lord to have a desire to come back. Where is the bride today? If the bride is not prepared, how can He come? If He were to come anyway, would He not come in vain? Only such a group of people who are constituted as the Lord's bride through practicing the new way will be able to bring in the Lord's return. I hope that we all will see this vision clearly.

We must be reminded here that we are going on in the way of recovery, beginning with the step of door-knocking. If we knock on the door of a Catholic or a Christian, we should never try to change them. No matter how much they praise, welcome, or admire you, they will almost always return to their own fold. Nevertheless, we must be broad and do our best to help them. Our strength, however, must be focused on the unbelievers or on the newly saved ones, setting up meetings in their homes and bringing them to know the truth. If we faithfully practice according to the principles we have fellowshipped, then in a year we will certainly double our number.

CHAPTER THREE

THE COMMISSION
TO CARRY OUT THE NEW WAY

THE COMMISSION OF GOD'S ECONOMY

The purpose of the practice of the new way is to practically carry out the gospel, truth, life, and the church, which God has commissioned us with. Our hope is that the new way would gain new ones, and that the new ones would walk in the new way.

Through more than sixty years of experience, during which we have carefully analyzed the practices of the Christian denominations and have studied the divine revelation again and again, we have found the way which is according to the Bible and ordained by God. This way is testified to and is according to the leading of the Holy Spirit, and it is most effective. We call it the "new way." Over the past two thousand years, there have been some who have seemingly taken this way but have not considered it to be the unique way ordained by God. Practically speaking, this new way has four steps. First, we go out knocking on doors and visiting people to preach the gospel and to lead them to be saved and baptized. After the experiments in the first term of the full-time training, this point has been proven to be workable. We have all heard the testimonies of the full-time trainees. There are even some who gained one hundred twenty people in a little more than two months and brought them to be baptized. This is a tremendous accomplishment.

Second, we must lead people into the knowledge of the truth. When we speak of the truth, we do not mean the ordinary, shallow truth spoken by most people, but the truth revealed in the Bible concerning God's eternal economy. God's eternal economy is that God in His Divine Trinity passed through various processes to dispense Himself into men that they may be regenerated, sanctified, renewed, transformed, conformed, and glorified to become the many members of Christ who constitute the Body of Christ as the corporate expression of God on earth. After we go out door-knocking to preach the gospel, we must establish meetings in the homes of all the newly baptized ones and begin to teach them this truth. This truth is the essence and the center of the Bible. This truth concerns what God intends to obtain according to His heart's desire. Christianity, however, has continually ignored this truth.

From my youth until the present, I have been studying the Bible for more than sixty-one years. The more I have studied it, the more I know the mystery it contains. This mystery is about God's eternal economy, which is truly a great matter. Within God there is an economy; by passing through various processes, He intends to dispense Himself into His chosen and redeemed people, uniting them with Himself as one entity and constituting them into the Body of Christ as the expression of God on earth. The saints should all study this truth thoroughly. They should understand it to the extent that they can open their mouths and easily teach it to the new ones. They should also make every new one someone who teaches others after just a few months of home meetings. If they do this, then in a very short time many people will know the truth of this mystery and all the other truths of the Bible. This is what we mean by our commission concerning the truth.

The truth includes all the riches of God with light, life, power, and all spiritual things. When we teach the truth to people, they will spontaneously be fed and supplied with life, and they will be able to grow in life. The life spoken of in the Bible refers to the uncreated, eternal life of God. This life is not something outside of or apart from God. This life is just God Himself. Therefore, this life is the Spirit, and the Spirit is Christ. When we say that we minister life to people, we mean that we minister the Spirit and Christ to them. Life, the Spirit, and Christ are all appositives referring to one substantial matter—the eternal life. Therefore, we should all jump with rejoicing because we have obtained this eternal life.

God, however, does not stop here. He has a unique purpose in dispensing His life into us. His intention is that we, the regenerated ones, may be sanctified, renewed, transformed, and conformed to the image of His firstborn Son and that we may be constituted as His Body, the church, the golden lampstands appearing in each locality to express His glory. Thus, our fourth commission is to build up the new ones—those who were baptized, have been edified in the truth, have grown in life, and are being transformed—into the Body of Christ as the corporate expression of God.

Most people consider Christianity a religion. In the Bible *religion* is a negative term, not a positive one. In other words, the Bible actually depreciates religion; religion has no position in the Bible. Therefore, is so-called Christianity really a religion? According to the orthodox, scriptural teaching, Christianity is actually not a religion. The suffix *-ianity* was brought in by translators. In the Bible there is only "Christ" without the "-ianity." Christ is a living Person who is the embodiment of the Triune God—the Father, the Son, and the Spirit—and who passed through death and resurrection to become the all-inclusive life-giving Spirit in order that we can breathe Him in and be filled and occupied by Him. I believe that when we meet together, He is with us, and He is also moving in many ways, giving grace to each one of us. This is the Christ mentioned in the Bible and the Christ whom we preach, believe, worship, and serve. He is not a religion, not even so-called Christianity; rather, He is the living Christ as the contents of our faith.

On the other hand, according to the degraded and deformed situation of Christianity, it has truly become a great religion, of which the largest sect is Catholicism and the second largest is Protestantism. In Protestantism, there are many denominations and sects. This is a universally recognized fact. May we all understand that we do not represent any kind or any sect of Christianity. We represent the church of God, which is the church as the living Body of Christ constituted with all the saints, that is, with all those who have His eternal life.

CARRYING OUT THE NEW WAY
FOR THE LORD'S COMMISSION

If we want to carry out the gospel, truth, life, and the church, then we must rely on the Holy Spirit and the word of God, and we must pray with all prayer and petition while laboring diligently. Over these past sixty years we have not been satisfied with the result of our experience. If we look back at the past two thousand years, the result of what Christianity has practiced has also been disappointing. Now the Lord has given us a definite new way for accomplishing His commission to us, which is the way of door-knocking, visiting people, establishing home meetings, teaching the truth, and bringing people into the building up of the church.

However, this kind of practice needs sufficient manpower. This is due to the fact that door-knocking is not an easy matter, visiting people is not a simple thing, teaching the truth and ministering life are even more difficult, and bringing people into the Body of Christ to live together in the practical church life is the most difficult of all. These matters will require not only time but also manpower. Therefore, after much prayer and study before the Lord, we have seen that if we are to carry out the Lord's commission, we will need three practical areas of coordination. First, those who meet regularly must produce one out of every twenty to be a full-time serving one who is supported by the other nineteen. Second, they must produce one out of every four to be a door-knocker who would spend at least two hours every week going out for door-knocking, caring for others, teaching the truth, fellowshipping with others, and ministering life. Third, in addition to the general offerings, everyone must give everything they have to support this move, not just with prayer but even more with monetary supply. This will be the strongest backing for this move.

Under normal circumstances, every full-timer who sets aside the Lord's Day for meeting and goes out six days for door-knocking and visiting people two to three hours a day will be able to gain at least one person each week for baptism. Those who go out two hours each week will be able to gain one person for baptism every two months. According to this principle, we will have a fourfold increase yearly. If we are faithful, this will not be merely wishful thinking but will be something attainable. I hope that we all will receive this commission and begin offering all that we can and all that we have for the gospel and for human souls.

THE ELDERS AND CO-WORKERS NEEDING TO BE PATTERNS OF THE FLOCK

The practice of the new way is not simple. Take door-knocking as an example. One person's door-knocking is different from another person's door-knocking. When a street-sweeper goes door-knocking, the feeling he gives others in his demeanor will be different from that of a college professor who goes door-knocking. In the same way, when the elders take the lead to go out door-knocking, they will be somewhat more weighty than most of the saints going out by themselves. Therefore, the elders must learn to lead. They should not be elders as in the former days, only sitting at a desk in the business office busying themselves with the miscellaneous affairs of the church. Instead, they should go out every day to knock on doors, care for people, teach people, and perfect people. Moreover, according to the Bible, the elders should not lord it over the flock but should become the leading sheep as patterns of the flock (1 Pet. 5:3). Likewise, the co-workers should take the lead to go out door-knocking. There should be no silent spectators among us. On the contrary, we should actively carry out these principles of twenty people producing one full-timer and four people producing at least one door-knocker. Moreover, all the saints should rise up to support, pray, and coordinate fully with monetary contributions so that the door-knockers, especially the full-time serving ones, can go forward with all their might without having to worry about their livelihood. Simultaneously, the co-workers and elders should take the lead to preach the gospel of the Lord's recovery, and all the saints should rise up as one man to allow the Lord to have the free way in this age to advance His economy.

THE PLAN TO EVANGELIZE TAIWAN IN FIVE YEARS

I am certain that if we faithfully go to practice and labor, the great project of evangelizing Taiwan in five years will be a success under the Lord's gracious leading. According to our original calculations, we would need two thousand five hundred full-timers for this evangelization project. Yet after our observations and experiences, at present I would say we need only one thousand to evangelize the entire island of Taiwan in the remaining few years. The brothers and sisters must pick up the burden to expend their energy by praying and offering their money for this matter so that the move to evangelize Taiwan, which began in 1985, can be accomplished by 1990.

If some full-time serving ones from other countries can participate in the move to evangelize and "churchize" Taiwan in five years, the results and the glory will be promising. We now have people of every color from the six continents on earth who have entered into this move. This is a very encouraging matter. I hope that the saints in all the local churches would say amen from the depths of their being to the Lord's new move today and that they would put forth their best effort to successfully carry out the unique, new way given to us by the Lord.

CHAPTER FOUR

THE PROPER CHRISTIAN SERVICE

THE SERVICE ACCORDING TO GOD'S WILL
MAKING THE BELIEVERS INWARDLY SATISFIED

By the Lord's mercy I was saved before I was twenty years old. After I was saved, I really loved the Lord, and I especially loved His Word, to such an extent that the Bible never left my hands. However, I had no place to meet because there was no meeting that could help me. Later I met with the Brethren Assembly and felt that it was not bad because they devoted themselves exclusively to expounding the Bible. I was very interested in this, so I followed them in their constant study. In those days, because I loved the Lord, it seemed that there was so much energy within me. Yet there was no outlet. At that time there was not the practical service. Nevertheless, every week I attended five meetings regularly and was not stopped by wind or rain. Sometimes it was very cold and snowing heavily, but I went to the meetings as usual. On one hand, such an experience was truly enjoyable. On the other hand, I did not have the slightest opportunity to function, nor was I involved in any service.

Thus, when I look back on my past experience, I have the deep realization that if a person is saved and loves the Lord but does not have the place or opportunity to serve the Lord and to function, then he will feel depressed and miserable. I believe that we have all had this experience. Although we may have shared something in the meetings, the more we continued with simply sharing, the more it seemed that all we could do was just this little bit, and inwardly we always felt unfulfilled and dissatisfied.

In John 4 the disciples went to buy food, and the Lord

Jesus sat alone beside a well. Eventually, He led a Samaritan woman to salvation. When the disciples returned, they said, "Rabbi, eat." The Lord said to them, "I have food to eat that you do not know about." The disciples were surprised and said to one another, "Has anyone brought Him anything to eat?" The Lord answered them, saying, "My food is to do the will of Him who sent Me and to finish His work" (vv. 31-34). I believe that many of us have a feeling of this kind: We go to meeting after meeting, listening to message after message, yet we feel as if a bowl of rice has been set before us but we have not eaten any of it. It was not until twenty years ago, when the Lord led us to begin the practice of pray-reading and to have the saints share at the end of the meetings, that we were able to have some enjoyment. At that time, the brothers and sisters felt it was truly enjoyable to stand up to share, and they would race to be the first. Gradually, however, we have been losing this taste.

I believe that most of us in the churches love the Lord, but we always feel as if something is missing. In our church life it seems as if there is a hole which we are unable to fill up. If I asked you whether or not you love the Lord, you would all certainly say that you do love Him. However, if I ask you if you feel satisfied, I am afraid you would all say that despite the fact that you meet frequently, have heard many messages, and share or testify regularly, you are still not satisfied inwardly. It seems there is so much energy within you, but there is no place in which you can use it, and there is so much vitality, but there is no outlet for it. You have no way to describe or explain these feelings. Now the church is changing the system to take the new way particularly for the sake of affording a way for that strong, inward impulse of love for the Lord to come out and so that we can be satisfied daily.

THE PROPER PRACTICE OF THE NEW WAY

Whoever has experienced this can testify that it is not good enough just to stand by and watch others go out door-knocking, visiting people, and leading them to be saved and baptized. Once you have led someone to be saved and baptized, however, you will jump for joy and be very satisfied. There is an elderly sister in the church in Anaheim who is more than seventy years old. After hearing about the practice of door-knocking, she tried it once and immediately gained one person for baptism. As a result, she has become "addicted" and feels as if she is floating on air. Whenever she meets people, she does not speak about anything else but how satisfied she is that she has gained a person through door-knocking.

Two weeks ago, an elder who came from a certain locality in America heard the messages about door-knocking and went out to knock on doors for two days; however, he did not gain a single person. Inwardly, he could not take it, and he went to the Lord to ask for the reason. Surprisingly, as soon as he prayed, he felt that he had to immediately make a thorough confession of his sins. So he did just that; he made a thorough confession of his sins. Afterward he went out door-knocking and gained two people. Now he also has become "addicted" and does not plan to return to America. He wants to stay to continue door-knocking.

Prayer along with a thorough confession of sins is a crucial point. Door-knocking is not a light matter. If you want to be effective, you must confess your sins. You should not do this in a superficial way; rather, you must thoroughly and completely confess your sins and totally empty yourselves so that you may be filled with the Holy Spirit. In this way your going out for door-knocking will certainly be effective.

TESTIMONIES OF SERVING
ACCORDING TO THE GOD-ORDAINED NEW WAY

There are two hundred fifty trainees from overseas, one hundred eighteen of whom have requested to stay in Taiwan. They cannot bear the thought of leaving so many whom they have gained through door-knocking and who need care. In one time of fellowship with the elders, a leading brother from America testified that he had attended a few home meetings since coming here and felt that they were very good. Now he does not feel satisfied unless he goes to a home meeting every evening. For this reason, I exhort all the elders and co-workers to taste this heavenly flavor first, to take the lead to go out door-knocking, and to attend the home meetings.

Furthermore, this new way is very effective. Not only are people gained quickly, but many of them also have a strong testimony. An eighty-six year old sister who was newly saved through door-knocking is very thankful that some of the trainees brought the gospel to her. In order to show her appreciation, she has given many snacks to the training center. Some other trainees knocked on a door last week and led the father of that household to salvation. When they went back this week, the son also received the Lord, and the father baptized him. There have also been cases in which the husband is saved one week and baptizes his wife the next week. Moreover, after this last conference meeting, one of the saints from America got lost and asked a policeman for help. All the way to the stadium he preached the gospel to that policeman. After arriving there, the policeman went in with him and was baptized. He also promised to have a meeting in his home. Such testimonies are very encouraging.

There was another sister who went out door-knocking for four days without gaining anyone, but she still went out patiently on the fifth day. On this day she gained a person who was baptized through her door-knocking. In a short time she gradually brought the five members of that family to be saved and baptized. Among these five was one young person who came to see her this afternoon, expressing a desire to attend the full-time training. There is not just one testimony like this; there are many. The young people whom these trainees have brought to the Lord are also willing to be like the trainees and to do what they do. This is a very sweet matter.

EVERYONE BEING A DOOR-KNOCKER

I believe that we all love the Lord and have inwardly aspired to serve the Lord. Now there is a way set before us through which we can realize our aspiration. Perhaps we will not all be full-timers, but we all can be door-knockers. This does not demand a great deal from us. We just need to be willing to go out for the Lord to knock on doors for two or three hours every week. There are one hundred sixty-eight hours in a week, and we need to consecrate only two or three hours, so this price is not too high. Do not think that we are so busy that we do not have time to spare. Actually we usually do things however we want and do not keep track of our time. For example, we read the newspapers as we like, chat with people as we please, and can be on the phone for a long time without feeling that our conversation is too long and without getting tired. It is only when we come to serve the Lord that we calculate the time carefully. This is the stratagem of the enemy.

This is why we must change our concept and act contrary to our natural disposition to force ourselves to set aside two or three hours a week for door-knocking, despite wind or rain. We should go out door-knocking week after week without ceasing. This is not at all a matter of whether or not we have time; rather, it is a matter of whether or not we are willing. If we are willing and if we care for this matter, then we will certainly have time to do it. Everyone likes to be free. Anything that one must do week after week becomes a burden. Even cleaning the house is like this. It takes ten minutes at the most to dust a table and no more than twenty or thirty minutes to vacuum the floor, but we may feel it is a burden to dust even weekly, much less daily. If there is no regulation and we are free to do whatever we like—making phone calls, reading newspapers, and going window-shopping as we please, not having to do a single thing that we dislike, then we will not feel anything is a burden. This is the condition of our natural man, so we truly need a strong turn. If we can all exercise to turn to our spirit and do things according to the feeling in our spirit, we will discover that going out door-knocking really is an opportunity given by the Lord for us to take a deep breath to fill up the empty hole within us.

DILIGENTLY LEARNING IN THE NEW WAY

The Lord has shown us that the church today is walking on an extraordinary, new way. Since it is an extraordinary way as well as a new way, much learning is needed for its practice. It is just like any technology, invention, or product of this modern age which requires serious training with practice before it can be used correctly. Take transportation, for example; it takes about one hundred days to walk from the east coast of America to the west coast. Everyone can walk, so learning is not required. As long as a person walks, he will arrive some day. However, if he wants to arrive more quickly, he must drive a car, and that takes much learning.

Likewise, when we bring up the matter of door-knocking, everybody knows how to do it. However, learning is necessary to do it correctly. Therefore, we will form teams by combining the regular saints and the trainees. In doing this we hope that the saints will learn from those who have already been trained. Door-knocking can be successful only if we are willing to humble ourselves and learn from others. It is a big mistake if we think that because we are older, it is easy for us to learn the new way by simply listening to a little explanation. Door-knocking involves many details; hence, we need to practice with the experienced ones so that by our personal experience we may learn the secret. In this way, we will soon taste the sweetness.

Many saved ones can testify that after they were baptized, they were really joyful. This corresponds with what the Bible says. Acts 8 says that when the Ethiopian eunuch was reading Isaiah 53, Philip was led by the Holy Spirit to approach his chariot and ask him, "Do you really know the things that you are reading?" He said, "How could I unless someone guides me?" Then he invited Philip to come into his chariot and explain it to him (Acts 8:27-31). They had not gone very far, and perhaps because Philip had talked to him about the matter of baptism, when the eunuch saw some water beside the road, he said, "Look, water. What prevents me from being baptized?" (v. 36). Philip did not delay either, and he immediately baptized the eunuch. The Holy Spirit does things in a marvelous way; as soon as the eunuch came up out of the water, the Holy Spirit caught Philip away, not leaving him with the eunuch. Still, the eunuch went on his way rejoicing (v. 39).

According to our old way of doing things, whenever we spoke of preaching the gospel, we first had to go out and invite people to come and hear the gospel. Then when they came, we were busy turning the pages of the Bible for them and helping them to listen to the message. After someone believed, we still did not let him get baptized immediately. First he had to attend four meetings on the truth of the gospel. Then we had to visit him in his home, and finally he had to have an interview for baptism. If the result of the interview was that he was unclear about the gospel truth, then he could not be baptized and had to wait for the next interview. He could be baptized only when he was clear about the gospel truth. Many times people were hindered from being saved because of such a delay.

The examples given to us in the Bible are not at all like this. In Acts 8, Philip preached the gospel to the eunuch, and in a very short time, perhaps only fifteen minutes, he baptized him. When Philip explained the passage in Isaiah, "As a sheep He was led to slaughter," he preached Jesus as the gospel through it. Immediately, when the eunuch saw some water, he wanted to be baptized. Therefore, Philip said, "If you believe from all your heart, you will be saved." The eunuch answered and said, "I believe that Jesus Christ is the Son of God" (vv. 30-37). Philip baptized him immediately.

According to our concept, after baptism there needs to be some edification of the new believers; otherwise, the new ones will not be able to stand firm. But after the eunuch was baptized, the Holy Spirit immediately caught Philip away without giving the eunuch the slightest chance to receive any edification. In the end, the eunuch returned to Ethiopia, which is a Gentile nation even today. This life pulse of the church has continued without break until this present day. Therefore, I exhort the elderly brothers and sisters to give up the old methods and learn this new way. It is like a military academy; the military teaching and training of forty or fifty years ago are useless today because everything has changed. This is why we say, "The new way gains new ones, and the new ones walk in the new way." We must be a new man—new both inwardly and outwardly—in order to be able to walk in the new way. We should not begin to walk in the new way and yet inwardly still be filled with the old things.

I want especially to mention the booklet called *The Mystery of Human Life*. When we go out door-knocking, we must take this booklet in addition to the Bible. After two years of use, it has been translated into all the languages spoken in the countries where there are churches in the Lord's recovery. This booklet speaks of the four keys for opening up the mystery of human life. We only need to learn how to speak according to this booklet, and we will obtain the secret. Whoever has the experience of going out door-knocking can testify that the more they speak according to the words in this booklet, the easier it is to bring people to be saved.

It used to be that baptizing people was not to be done carelessly; rather, baptism had to be carried out by the elders. However, sometimes when a person had to wait, he would wait so long that he disappeared. In the northern Chinese dialect we have a very interesting expression called *huo ho,* which means "optimum cooking temperature." This Chinese expression means that when we do something, we must seize the best opportunity. We may compare this to a housewife who heats the oil in the wok to just the right temperature and prepares to stir-fry some vegetables, but delays for three minutes in order to answer the phone; as a result, the vegetables do not taste as good as they should. In the same way, we should lead a person to baptism once he believes in the Lord. If there is a waiting period, then his baptism may be frustrated. The Bible says to believe and be baptized (Mark 16:16). It is a spontaneous matter to baptize someone immediately after he has believed.

I was the one who designed and taught our previous way of practice, including the interview for baptism and the procedure for baptism, so I am the one best qualified to overthrow it, and I should overthrow it. In the past we rode in ox carts, so I certainly had to teach you how to ride in an ox cart. Now we have changed our mode of transportation to the automobile, so we should not do things in the same way as when we used carts. Rather, we should learn the new way; we should learn to drive an automobile. We should not think of driving oxen while riding in an automobile even though we are accustomed to driving oxen. In the past when the women sewed or embroidered, they did it all stitch by stitch. Now they have sewing machines, but they may think that the clothes they make do not look nice enough. Actually, the problem is that they are not attentive enough when using the sewing machine. If we are really willing to humble ourselves and diligently learn anew, rejecting our old habits and customs, then we will certainly do things faster and better.

It is very hard to change one's concept. I myself have been making the turn for five years. From 1980 to 1984 I was constantly studying why in the Lord's recovery we would preach the gospel and labor hard every year, but our numbers would not increase. It was not only like this in Taiwan; it was also the same in the United States. This question pressed me until I had no other way but to return to the Bible and spend time studying it diligently. In the end the Lord showed me the concept of the "home." According to the revelation of the Bible, God Himself came down from heaven to be incarnated and at His own discretion went from one home to another to seek sinners. The Lord Himself went to the home of Zaccheus. He also made a special trip to seek the sinful woman by the well in Samaria. The New Testament clearly shows us that the home is the center and that the gospel is a matter of being delivered to the home and not a matter of inviting people to come and listen. If today God were to invite us to where He sits in the heavens, we would never find a way to get there. Instead, He came down and brought the gospel to us, making it so available for us. Because we have acted against this principle, we have not had the Lord's blessing for a long time.

When I saw this clearly, I made a thorough repentance to the Lord. Thirty years ago when I was still living in Taiwan, I saw people riding bicycles with a sign that said, "Delivering Shots to Your Home." This meant that a person did not have to go to the doctor's clinic, but the doctor would come to the person's home and give him the shot. Now America has home delivery services for food which make it very helpful for business. If you make it convenient for people, they will welcome you. In the same way, if our hope is that the Lord's recovery will increase and spread, then we must change our concept. Instead of inviting people to come and hear the gospel, we should deliver the gospel to their homes. This will help us to increase.

THE PRACTICAL AND DETAILED WAY
FOR DOOR-KNOCKING

There is a practical and detailed way to do anything, and as long as we copy it exactly, studying and practicing according to the pattern, we will be able to do the thing in the right way. Before we go out door-knocking, we must dress properly. Our appearance should not be too conservative, nor should it be too modern and stylish. Rather, it should be neat and proper, serious and appropriate. Even our hair must be brushed and tidy. If we do this, people will open their doors to us. Suppose three people are in a group to go out door-knocking; one is an American hippie with long hair and an unkempt beard, another one is a Taiwanese hoodlum with shoes but no socks, and the third one is a Hong Kong gangster holding a cigarette in his mouth and wearing a pair of dark glasses. When these three persons go out door-knocking, people will certainly be frightened and think that they are there to rob them or to do some other evil thing; they would definitely not open the door to them. But if the same three persons go out door-knocking with a clean and neat appearance, wearing proper clothing and walking in a proper way, then people will certainly open their doors and welcome them.

Practicing to build up a proper, neat character is the topic of a required course in our full-time training. The trainees are required to go to bed early and to get up early. Every morning they have to straighten their rooms and have morning watch, then they go out jogging for bodily exercise. Once the training center asked all the trainees to put their shoes outside their bedroom doors before they went to sleep. The seven hundred fifty trainees fearfully did as they were told. After the trainees had gone to sleep, the trainers came and polished their shoes until they were bright and shiny. The next morning after rising, the trainees saw that all their shoes were black and shiny; they were both touched and ashamed. Because of this kind of training, the character of the trainees has been gradually built up to the extent that they can gain others as soon as they go out. Therefore, if we want to participate in the hosts of Calvary to go out door-knocking to gain people, the first thing we must do is have a proper appearance.

Next, our attitude must be one of humility and courtesy. We need to be humble and courteous to people, especially in our speech. Therefore, the training also teaches us how to speak properly. Do not think that the training only teaches the skill of door-knocking. The training is mainly for teaching us what to say and what to do when preaching the gospel so that people will be open to receive. Thus, the first requirement is a neat appearance and the second is an attitude of humility and courtesy. These two things are outward matters.

Concerning the inward matters, the intrinsic thing is that when we go out door-knocking, we must pray first and we must pray thoroughly, confessing our sins, repenting, and being filled by the Lord. If we are not filled with the Lord inwardly but have only given ourselves a proper outward appearance, then we are only actors putting on a show with stage make-up, and what we do is not of any value. Therefore, we must have thorough prayer and be filled with the Lord inwardly, then we must have a proper outward appearance before we will be ready to go out door-knocking.

Moreover, we must learn how to coordinate together. We should never choose the ones with whom we coordinate. When the training or the church assigns the teams, we should not choose to be with the people we like. Usually when we go out door-knocking there are three people to a team with one elderly person, one middle-aged person, and one young person. The function of the elderly person is not to speak but to knock on the doors. This is very valuable. After the door has been opened, the young saint should open his mouth and introduce himself. After getting inside the door, the elderly saint is responsible for standing to the side to nod and smile in support, while the young brothers and sisters are responsible for explaining the truth. This seems to be the opposite of the worldly way, but it is very effective.

If a person gets saved and wants to be baptized, it is best for the elderly brother to pray and do the baptizing because he is weightier and more experienced. People will feel more at peace receiving it from him. But if there is an elderly sister present, she should help prepare the water and the clothing and just assist on the sidelines during the baptism. We must pay attention to all these little points. We should never think that it is all right to ignore them. They can have a great influence on what we are doing.

When the working saints go out door-knocking, they should mainly learn to speak. Do not speak your own words. Speak what the training teaches you to speak. Therefore, you must pay particular attention to the preaching and speaking of the trainees in order to learn from them. Furthermore, you should coordinate together to go into the houses, and to sit with people while they are listening, praying, and being baptized. Learn a few times and you will do well in the end.

LEARNING THE NEW WAY FOR OUR SERVICE

In conclusion, for many years in the church life we have been loving the Lord, attending meetings, serving in various areas, reading the Bible, and praying, but within us there has always been a feeling that something is lacking. Now with the practice of the new way, we have been given the opportunity and the way to serve that can fill up our inward lack. Therefore, we must seize this opportunity. Second, the new way is focused on the individual homes, and its practice has four definite steps. The first step is to go out door-knocking and to baptize people; the second step is to establish a home meeting immediately in the new ones' homes; the third step is to teach the truth in the homes to build up the new ones in the habits of reading the Bible and prayer. In this way they will not repeat our mistake of listening to others give messages for thirty years without being edified or understanding the truth. On the other hand, we also need teachers to teach the new ones and to help them to properly use the lesson books. These teachers, however, should not teach according to their own opinions. Instead, they should teach in a living, interesting, and weighty manner in order to supply the new ones. The fourth step is to bring the new ones into the knowledge and living of the practical church life. In the end, they will not just be baptized; they will learn the truth in their homes to be supplied and grow in life. They will also live in the practical church life and coordinate together in the service.

At present, we already have more than one thousand home

meetings. Although many of us have picked up the burden to become door-knockers, we should not go to the homes of the new ones to "lead" a home meeting. Instead, we should go to meet together with the new ones and teach them to do what we do. This will be the only way for us to continue increasing and spreading.

The Bible clearly reveals that God's economy has the home as its focus. The controlling vision of our change of system is to take the focus off the meetings and place it onto the homes. Our hope is not that the new ones would be saved and immediately come to the meetings. We also do not want to continue building meeting halls in every place. Once there is a meeting hall, then an organization might be produced, and it may gradually turn into a situation in which one person speaks and everyone else listens. This would be going back to a condition under the influence of Christianity's old way. If there are no meeting halls but only home meetings, it will be easy for everyone to function. However, we cannot have the church life only in the homes. There is still a need for all the saints to be connected and joined together (Eph. 4:16). Thus, we are still researching into a properly balanced way. I ask you all to pray for this matter and to do your best to cooperate in thoroughly changing from the old way to the new way. This will not only give the saints the opportunity and way to function, but also it will bring in the real multiplication and increase to carry out God's economy.

CHAPTER FIVE

HOW TO CARE FOR NEW ONES THROUGH THE HOME MEETINGS

According to the statistics, there are 500,000 households in all of Taipei. In this past year we have knocked on the doors of 150,000 households, and the number of people baptized through door-knocking is more than 5,700. We rejoice because the more we go out door-knocking, the more effective we are. For example, in the most recent time of door-knocking there were 321 people who went out, and the result was that 157 were saved and baptized.

THE HOMES AS PILLARS SUPPORTING THE CHURCH

Going out to knock on doors to bring people to salvation, establishing home meetings in the homes of the new ones, and teaching them to read the Bible and pray are just the initial steps. In the same way, a baby still needs a lot of nourishment and care after its birth. We all know that if a child is to grow up to maturity, after it is born, it needs to be nourished and taught. It is easy to give birth, but it is not so easy to nourish, and it is even more difficult to teach. Therefore, we must look at these things point by point to see how to carry out the proper nourishing and teaching. We will begin with the homes as a starting point.

We need to come back to the Scriptures to see the matter of meeting in the homes. For more than fifty years I have been studying the practices recorded in the Bible concerning the way for Christians to meet. The Bible does not have a clear word concerning this point; it shows us only a few patterns. Concerning the meetings, Hebrews 10:25 says that we should not abandon our own assembling together, and 1 Corinthians

14:26 tells us what things we should do when the whole church comes together, but it does not explain how to do them. These two passages are both words of teaching. The patterns given to us in the Bible are mainly in the book of Acts. Acts tells us that the early church met in the homes, from house to house (2:46; 5:42; 12:12).

Thus, according to this small but penetrating light in the Bible, the earliest church life was entirely carried out in the homes. It was altogether not like the situation today. Today there are a great many church buildings everywhere but few proper, living home meetings. I dare not say that they are absolutely nonexistent, but I can say that there is nothing concrete. In the age of the apostles, as soon as the church was formed, several thousand people were immediately brought to salvation. One time there were three thousand, and another time there were five thousand (2:41; 4:4). Then they simply met from house to house. When they met, they did mainly four things: preach the gospel, teach the truth, pray, and break bread. This is the light of revelation in the Bible, the clear leading of the Holy Spirit, and even more, the proper practice ordained by God.

Due to the degradation of the church, this kind of condition was gradually lost. As a result, organized Christianity was formed. Once there was organization, the result was the establishing of large corporate meetings, followed by the need for preachers. After the organization, the officers, and the preachers were brought forth, the clergy was produced. Once there was the clergy, the believers were divided into classes. Those belonging to the clergy were the speakers, while those belonging to the non-clergy were the listeners. Thus, Christian service and functioning in the meetings were completely taken over by a small number of people. Even today this kind of situation still exists everywhere, especially in Catholicism. Most Catholics know only to go to mass, but they are not able to perform any function as members. The situation in Protestantism is also like this.

As far as we are concerned, the situation in Taipei a few years ago was just about the same. We frequently had large meetings with just a few people doing everything. This kind of condition made me very concerned. Therefore, I received a burden from the Lord and saw that we must overturn these things. The first thing we must do is to overturn the big meetings.

However, I do not have the intention of entirely stopping the big meetings. Changing the system should not be like jumping from the seventh floor straight to the ground floor, without using stairs at all; that is to commit suicide. Rather, for the past two years we have been changing the system and simultaneously building a staircase on which all the saints can walk down properly instead of lingering on the seventh floor with a wait-and-see attitude. What we have seen before the Lord is that one day in the Lord's recovery there will be mostly home meetings and not many big meetings. Perhaps once or twice a month the whole church will come together for a meeting like the one mentioned in 1 Corinthians 14. That will be such a glorious situation!

In the past we had a meeting at a big stadium with ten thousand people, which was marvelous and impressive. However, if there were no home meetings as supporting pillars, that kind of big meeting would not be a glory but a deformity. We must have home meetings before we can have big meetings. Our labor is not in the big meetings but in the home meetings. It is only after we have constantly labored in the home meetings that one day we can have a big meeting as a harvest. This is the same as the children of Israel celebrating the Feast of Tabernacles after laboring throughout the entire year to obtain a harvest which they enjoyed as a feast before God when they came together. It is also like the American Thanksgiving Day which was originally celebrated after the harvest was taken in; the families gathered together to enjoy the fresh produce in their homes. Perhaps we could follow the children of Israel to have three big meetings in each year of labor and work. These would be times of joy and exultation.

This is why we must change our concepts. I say again that we are not jumping off a building and committing suicide; rather, we are willing to turn around and walk down the stairs. Instead of finding excuses for yourself, you should follow everyone else down the stairs. The Chinese all used to wear long gowns, but today it is difficult to find anyone in a gown, because everyone is now wearing Western clothes. This proves that people can change. Even though it is difficult to come down the stairs, as long as we are willing to walk, we will be able to slowly get down to the ground floor.

If we are to walk, however, we must change our concept. In the past our Lord's Day meetings had two or three hundred people, and the speakers were all experienced and spoke every sentence well and in a touching way, so that even the gospel friends were helped. Now as we are changing the system, the big meetings have become small and the saints are scattered. Moreover, our baptisms are not what they used to be, with baptism interviews to determine if the candidates are clearly saved before we baptize them. Now we just need to preach *The Mystery of Human Life* to them, lead them in prayer, and baptize them in the bathtub after they have believed. It seems that the change in system is turning the church into a mess. Please do not be worried. Instead, you must wait patiently. I believe that after three to five years many homes will have been raised up as the supporting pillars of the church.

Things in the physical world are symbols of things in the spiritual realm. A country's strength and a society's health are entirely determined by the strength and health of the families. According to the Chinese tradition, the children are raised by the parents in the homes; they are taught, they live, and they grow up at home. Then after they are married, they do not need to ask an expert on "family-forming" for guidance. They know spontaneously how to form a family and build up a career. This is because they have been with their parents since they were small and therefore have a thorough understanding of what a family is all about. This is just what we have seen before the Lord. The Christian "society"—the church—is not composed of church buildings. Rather, it is constituted with households. The household is the basic unit of salvation and service, and it is the constituting element of the church.

TAKING THE HOME AS THE CENTER
TO BRING IN THE FUNCTIONING OF ALL THE MEMBERS

We can bring everyone into function by taking the home as the center. According to the modern way of life, no household hires a cook to do all the cooking for the family. If there are such households they are a small minority. More than thirty years ago, it was very easy to hire servants to keep house and do the cooking. Now, due to the increase in the cost of labor, almost every household cooks for itself and does all the housework itself. The result is that the households are becoming stronger and stronger. Today when Christians consider spiritual devotion and edification, they have to hire a speaker to hold an edification meeting or they do not know how to go on. We hope that after going through a thorough change of system, we will no longer have the thought of hiring a speaker because everyone will be able to speak and carry out all the service in the meetings. This kind of meeting will certainly be strong and rich. If the saints are willing to change their concept and receive the practice of changing the system, I believe that after just a few years all will be drawn by the home meetings. Moreover, everyone will feel that a large meeting in which one person speaks and everyone else listens has lost its flavor. In the past we listened to one person speaking in the meeting hall. After listening for all those years, even though we cannot say that the messages we heard were the conventional sermons of ordinary Christianity, we can say that they were the "conventional" teachings of the local churches. In a few years, however, I believe that in Taipei we will have several thousand homes in which there are meetings and activities. The participants in these meetings will all be able to speak and function and even their children will be able to lead others to sing hymns.

THE FIRST STEP
FOR THE SUCCESS OF THE NEW WAY

In order for us to arrive at the glorious future we are describing, we must spend our time and energy. Up to the present, everyone has learned well how to go out door-knocking and lead people to be baptized. In ten minutes you can bring a person to be saved, and in fifteen minutes you can get him baptized. In the past even I would not have believed this was possible, and probably you would not either. Doctrinally speaking, we always feel that baptism should not be so fast. In the Bible, however, there definitely is the clear revelation that no person after believing in the Lord has to wait and attend gospel truth meetings, then pass through a baptism interview in which he has to be absolutely clear about salvation before getting baptized. The only person who was delayed in getting baptized was Paul; in this he was a special case. Therefore, when Ananias was sent by the Lord to carry out the baptism, he said to Paul, "And now, why do you delay? Rise up and be baptized...calling on His name" (Acts 22:16). This is why we should no longer ask people to wait. If a person believes but then wants to wait, we should point this verse out to him and tell him that he should not delay but should be baptized immediately. This is the first step for the success of the new way.

Moreover, most people have the concept that baptism is a very solemn matter which should be carried out at the meeting hall. Acts 8 gives a very clear example about the Ethiopian eunuch, a person who greatly desired to understand the Word and who after hearing the gospel immediately requested to be baptized when he saw a place with water. He was not even baptized in a bathtub; it was perhaps just a pool, a puddle, or a stream of water on the roadside (vv. 36-38). You should not think that a person baptized in this way is probably not reliable. This eunuch is the best testimony.

THE EQUIPPING NEEDED
FOR LEADING A HOME MEETING

The second step of the new way is leading the home meetings. It is very simple for someone to lead a large meeting, because he just has to follow a certain procedure step by step and everything will go well. It is not so simple, however, to lead a home meeting. We must be properly equipped if we desire to take the lead in a home meeting. First, we must be those who love the Lord to such an extent that like Mary we are willing to break our flask of alabaster for the Lord.

Next, we must be those who pray and fellowship with the Lord. Loving the Lord is not a slogan; it must be expressed in a practical way. If we really love the Lord, we will certainly have fellowship and be in union with Him every day. We will tell Him, "Lord, I belong to You. I love You." Inwardly, we will always have a feeling that although our body is in the world, we are neither of the world nor for the world. Although I am an old man, I still frequently say, "Lord Jesus, I love You." Every time I think of Him and call His name, I am so rapturous, as if I am flying in the air, and I feel sweet and refreshed. This is the spontaneous living of one who loves the Lord. Even though we might still go to work, do our business, or study as usual, we are different from others because inwardly we have nothing but the Lord Jesus. The only things we think about and care for are the Lord and His interests.

Next, we must be those who read the Lord's Word. In order to lead the home meetings, we must be equipped with the Lord's Word. It should not be that we read it only when we are interested, and if we are not interested, we do not touch it for three months. Instead, we must read it regularly every day to enjoy the Spirit and life in the Lord's Word daily. Inwardly we all hate sin and desire to be freed from sin. We were born in sin, our nature is sin, and the environment around us is all sin, so it is not so easy for us to be completely delivered from sin. However, because of the Lord's love, we desire to be freed from sin. When we feel that we have been contaminated, we can apply the Lord's precious blood and ask God to forgive and wash away our sins based on our confession and according to His faithfulness and righteousness (1 John 1:7, 9). Thus, we live before the Lord and are joined to Him every day by loving Him, fellowshipping with Him, praying to Him, reading His Word, hating sin, and confessing our sins with repentance.

In this way, the Lord's presence in us will be rich and increasing, and the Lord will give us a burden to love the brothers and sisters and the people in the world. This is like the call which the Lord gave at the Sea of Tiberias: "Do you love Me more than these? Feed My lambs. Shepherd My little sheep" (John 21:16-17). Do we love the Lord? If we really love

Him, we should go to our friends' and neighbors' homes and minister Him to them. There are so many people in the world who have not heard the gospel. We must preach the Lord Jesus to them. This is the burden given to us by the Lord, and we must receive it.

After we have been equipped in the matters mentioned above, we will be qualified to go out door-knocking. In addition, there is one thing that we must pay attention to; we must learn from those who know how to go out door-knocking. Everything has its technique or secret, so we must learn. The Bible also tells us to learn. Paul reminded Timothy that he should know from whom he had learned things (2 Tim. 3:14). He also exhorted Timothy to take the things he had heard from Paul and commit them to faithful men, who would be competent to teach others also (2:2). However, if we do not first have the proper equipping mentioned above, even if we learn all the techniques, it will be useless. We will be like monkeys imitating humans, having only an outward show but no life, and therefore will not be able to truly minister to people.

The Chinese say, "There are no teachers of great masters, only students of great masters." If we want to be like "students of the great masters," besides loving the Lord, being joined to Him, and fellowshipping with Him, we must daily read the Word, pray, hate sin, confess our sins, and deal with sins. We must also receive a burden from the Lord to preach the gospel and be willing to learn from those who know.

From my youth I studied in American schools and learned the customs of my teachers, but in my hometown I did not dare speak English or wear Western clothes for fear of being criticized. More than thirty years ago I came to Taiwan to begin the Lord's work. When I gave messages on the platform, I still wore the Chinese long gown and short jacket. Now, however, those who criticized others have also changed and are all wearing Western clothes. They have received the new things. In the same way, I believe that in thirty years Taipei will be filled with home meetings, and all will be functioning, all will open their mouths, and all will be able to do these things that we are now doing. They will be born into this way and will be raised up and grow in this way, so they will be able to do the same things.

THE KEY TO LEADING THE HOME MEETINGS

A Definite Goal—Evangelizing the Entire Earth

There are some saints who are unable to go out door-knocking because they are elderly, but they are concerned about the effectiveness of practicing the new way. They are worried that the young people will be too careless when they go to people's homes to baptize people. However, the Lord's blessing surpasses whatever we can ask or think. I have the assurance and faith that this is definitely the proper, God-ordained way of blessing. As long as we are certain of our goal to evangelize the world by first evangelizing Taiwan, which means first evangelizing Taipei, and as long as our way is proper, then I deeply believe that the goal of God's economy will be realized by us one day in the near future.

For this reason, the full-time trainees must learn foreign languages, especially English and Greek. English is the international language of the world, and Greek is the original language of the New Testament. These are two required courses for anyone who would serve the Lord. Other languages such as German, French, Spanish, and Japanese should be electives. These are a preparation for the evangelization and "truthizing" of the entire world.

Our Tools—the Word and the Spirit

At present, our greatest need is to learn how to lead the home meetings. The first step—door-knocking, leading people to believe, and baptizing them—is being adeptly and properly done by the trainees. But they are still searching for the way to lead the home meetings. According to my study, no matter what we do, we must have the proper tools and methods. We cannot lack either of these things. Our "tools" clearly consist of two items: the Word of God—the Bible—and the Spirit of God. The Chinese have a saying, "Good tools are prerequisite to the successful execution of a job." If we are to lead the home meetings, we first need to be equipped with a store of the

Lord's word. Not only should we read the Bible, but we should also read the spiritual books in the Lord's recovery to help us know such things as God's economy, the dispensing of the Triune God, and the mystery of human life.

Studying depends on our heart. If we want to know the truth, we must set our hearts on the truth and spend much time in thorough study. Even though most people say they do not have enough time to read, I would still suggest that you learn to grasp the odd moments throughout the day. You should place books like the Bible, the life-studies, and *Truth Lessons* all over your house so that you can use your time well by reading at any time in any place. There is a saying, "Whenever you open a book, you will be benefitted." If you read much, you will spontaneously love to read. I hope that we all could read the Bible and the ministry books to such an extent that we would read only the headlines of the newspapers and not be interested in watching television; we would read the Lord's word with great relish. Although we still have to work, eat, and carry on our daily routine as usual, we can still do our best to grasp each extra moment and diligently read the Word. This will help us to have intimate fellowship with the Lord and to obtain a good supply from the Lord. In this way the Lord's word will be gradually deposited into our inward parts until it saturates our being, so that all we think about is just His word and all we speak will spontaneously also be just His word. When we go out to knock on doors or to lead a home meeting, we will be able to boldly speak and minister the Lord's word.

The second "tool" for leading the home meetings is the Holy Spirit, who is the Lord Himself. Today the worldly religion either has the demonic spirits or is without any spirit, but we have the Holy Spirit. God is Spirit, and the third of the Divine Trinity is the Spirit. The Lord Jesus as the Son also passed through death and resurrection to be transfigured into the Spirit. Consummately, God leads us by being such a Spirit who indwells us. I am more than eighty years old and I am still here laboring with all my strength. The saints often worry about me, and my wife especially is afraid that I will be too tired. Instead of feeling tired, however, I have been strengthened by working more because I have the covering and supply of the Lord's Spirit.

When we love the Lord, are joined to the Lord, draw near to Him, fellowship with Him, read His Word, hate sins, and confess our sins as soon as we have been contaminated, then this pneumatic Lord is with us in our experience. He is one with us and He is in us, speaking and acting together with us. Thus, when we go out to knock on doors and lead the home meetings, we must first believe that He speaks when we speak, and He moves when we minister to others. At the same time, we must also pray and ask the Lord to speak in our speaking, telling the Lord that we would speak only when He speaks.

Many times when we speak for the Lord we are not so eloquent, but people truly are supplied. Actually, this is not our doing but the working of the Word and the Spirit within us. When we speak God's word, the Word of God, which is Spirit and life, supplies people with the Spirit and life. As a result, when people hear it, they are infused with the divine element. The Word and the Spirit are our "tools." For this reason, the full-timers must confess their sins daily in order to be filled with the Holy Spirit. If we confess thoroughly to the Lord, the Holy Spirit will definitely fill us. Do not think that being filled with the Holy Spirit just means speaking in tongues. Rather, being filled with the Holy Spirit will give us faith and make us able to minister to others. Maybe we are not perfect, but we believe and we are able. In saying this, we are not deceiving ourselves and others. Rather, this is based on fact. When we have thoroughly confessed our sins and emptied ourselves completely, the Lord is surely with us and the Holy Spirit surely fills us. Consequently, we will have the Word and the Spirit.

Two Ways—Praying and Singing

There are two "tools" for leading a home meeting: the Word and the Spirit. There are also two ways for leading a home meeting: praying and singing. Concerning praying, we should pray as soon as we enter the meeting and also lead others to pray; however, we should not pray in a routine or perfunctory way. Concerning singing, we may not have any musical ability and are out of tune when we sing, but this is not important. What is important is that we must sing. Praying and singing are two ways necessary for leading the home meetings.

There is a secret to these two ways. The secret is that we must be "crazy" in our spirit (cf. 2 Cor. 5:13; Acts 26:24-25). We must be "crazy" when we pray and "crazy" when we sing. When we go out to lead the home meetings, we must be a "crazy" person. Like someone who is drunk, we are full of new wine and filled with the Holy Spirit. This requires us to be those who pray and praise all the time. Do not care about or be limited by the circumstances. For example, sometimes when we visit a home, there are only little children there. This is not a problem. We can lead them to sing, "Since Jesus came into my heart," while we wait for the mother to come home. If her face is not too happy when she returns, we should not be affected. On the contrary, we should be filled in spirit and sing, "O let us rejoice in the Lord evermore." Thus, we will be able to minister to them through singing.

You should know that a person with the leading and presence of the Holy Spirit is like "one who is beside himself." When we are "crazy" and "drunk" in spirit, the Holy Spirit will be with us. If we are not at all filled with the Holy Spirit and are like old men sitting as stable as a great mountain, then the Holy Spirit will have no way to do anything. The Holy Spirit has no way to move those who are immovable and rigid. Only those who are open can be moved by the Holy Spirit. Whether a meeting is living or dead totally depends on whether we are living or dead. If we are living and beside ourselves, even a dead meeting will become living because of us.

We must be those who are "crazy" in spirit in order to lead others to be "crazy" in spirit. If we want to help people not to be formal in prayer, then we must pray "crazy" prayers instead of conventional prayers. We must be like Paul, who was like a "pest" and a "plague" and was able to stir people up and "infect" them (Acts 24:5). Our whole being must be full of "germs," so that when we contact people, we immediately "infect" them with the "germs" and make them "crazy" too. If we are this kind of person, when we lead the home meetings, we will make others this kind of person also. This is to escape from the degradation of Christianity and to completely repudiate the degraded customs of Christianity. In this way the home meetings will be full of the enjoyment of God and the presence of the Lord.

PERFECTING IN THE HOME MEETINGS

God gave the natural world a law of "each after its own kind" (cf. Gen. 1:11-25). If we are white, our children will look like us; and if we are black, our children will also look like us. It is unusual for parents to give birth to a child that does not look like them. If we possess certain characteristics, then we cannot avoid passing them on to our children. In the same principle, we will cause the people whom we are caring for to be the same as we are. If we love the Lord and His word, if we are always filled with the Holy Spirit—praying and singing livingly and crazily—then when we go to lead the home meetings, we will certainly cause people to be supplied and to love the Lord. As a result, the world will spontaneously fall away from them and they will not want anything other than the Lord and His word.

Therefore, when we go to lead a home meeting, we should have these four items—the Lord's Word, the Holy Spirit, praying, and singing—as our foundation. We should be acquainted with the Word, be rich in the Word, and have a thorough understanding of the Word. We should be constantly, richly filled and overflowing with the Spirit. We should pray and sing in a crazy and living way. The Word, the Spirit, praying, and singing are four keys to leading the home meetings. The Word and the Spirit are "tools," while praying and singing are ways. The Word and the Spirit are the base, while praying and singing are the expression.

OVERTURNING OUR CONCEPT BEING NECESSARY FOR EVANGELIZATION

However, we do not only emphasize ways and techniques; rather, through these ways and techniques we are overturning everyone's concepts to rid ourselves of all that is old, even old feelings, flavors, and thoughts, until we are inwardly filled with the home meetings. We use home meetings to preach the gospel, speak the truth, and feed others. We pray and break bread in the homes in order to make the home meetings the practical church life. If our concept is completely changed, if, according to the principle we set forth, we produce a full-timer for every twenty saints and a weekly door-knocker for every four saints, and if all the saints continue to support and give their all to preach the gospel house to house, then I believe that within three to five years we can produce a completely new generation. This could comprise more than ten thousand households and sixty or seventy thousand new ones who meet regularly and who go everywhere preaching the gospel and teaching the truth. This will bring in a genuine great revival.

Door-knocking to preach the gospel is not only the God-ordained way but also the best way according to the needs of human society. Man is a social creature, and every human being likes to be part of a group, but it is not easy to find a good and proper social group. The church is the best "society" because we give people salvation and the Lord as life. This brings great blessing to a person's family. Today one of the greatest problems in American families is that many of the young people, including junior high and elementary school students, take drugs. However, by the Lord's preserving, this problem is almost non-existent among the children of our brothers and sisters in the church because they receive the protection of the truth. The Chinese proverb says, "He who nears vermilion becomes red; he who nears ink becomes black." This is a natural outcome. This is also why we continually emphasize that the household is the unit for receiving blessings. We must stress the home meetings.

I believe that the day will come when the gospel will not be preached just by those of us who are here; instead, it will be preached by all the brothers and sisters because everyone will be able to preach effectively and the rate of increase will be high. In the meetings it will not be just a few people who are functioning, but everyone will be full of the Lord's Word and the Spirit and will function in a living and fresh way. This is true evangelization.

CHAPTER SIX

HOW TO TEACH THE NEW ONES
IN THE HOME MEETINGS

THE PROPER CHURCH LIFE BEING BUILT UP
IN THE HOME MEETINGS

The Lord wants us to practice His ordained way with the ultimate result of bringing the church life completely into the homes. The Bible gives us such a pattern in Acts. After the apostles passed away, however, the church, affected by various tests, fell into the condition of today's Christianity. Instead of having the church life in the homes, the believers hold big meetings in large worship halls with one person speaking and all the rest listening. If the big meetings were eliminated, Christianity would be finished. We hope that according to what we have seen in the Bible, we could bring the church life back into the homes in the shortest time possible. In this way the church will still be able to prosper and go on even without the big meetings.

Just like a society or a nation, the basic factor of the church's health is the family. If each family is strong, all the problems will be solved. If the families are not doing well, then the problems in society cannot be solved, and the proper persons cannot be produced to be the steadying strength of society. If a nation or society wants to produce useful people, it cannot rely merely on education. Rather, it must rely on healthy families because the family is its supporting strength.

Let us take Taiwan as an example. The progress of these past few years has been possible for the undeniable reason that the families are healthy. For the sake of building up the families and perfecting their children, the parents in Taiwan all go to work early and come home late, labor diligently, and live thriftily to have some savings for supporting their families. They mainly pay attention to the education of their children, considering the perfecting of their children to be one of the most important things in life. They even do certain things themselves in order to be a pattern to their children. This is because they know that if the family is not strong, their children will not be able to receive a sufficiently high level of education to have a secure future. Their concept of society is not necessarily strong, nor are they always patriotic, but their concept of the family is deep and strong. They firmly believe that the family is the stabilizing force of everything, the cause and factor of progress, and that if they do not take care of the family, then society and the country will be finished. This is an important factor in Taiwan's becoming stable and prosperous.

The main function of the family is not to beget children. Begetting children is not a problem; people start begetting as soon as they are married. After the begetting, however, the nourishing and educating are great sciences. A proper family must carry out the begetting, the nourishing, and the educating simultaneously. Although we rely on the schools for a large portion of the education of our children, it is difficult for the schools to produce good students without the support of good families. Good students are cultivated by good families.

Nearly the entire supporting strength of all Christianity today is in the big meetings. They invite famous people to preach sermons and hire pastors with degrees, special talents, and eloquence who can gather, contact, and organize people. The result is that the strength of the meetings and the shepherding of the believers depends solely on the pastor. If the pastor leaves, the meetings collapse, and the believers lose their care and nourishing. Therefore, this practice of relying only on the big meetings is truly not the proper way revealed in the Bible. The Bible shows us that the proper church life must be carried out and built up in the homes.

RECEIVING A BURDEN TO CARE FOR AND NOURISH THE NEW ONES IN THE HOME MEETINGS

The first step for practicing the new way, the God-ordained

way, is to knock on doors and bring people to be saved and baptized. The second step is to set up meetings in the new ones' homes to feed and care for them. We can say that the practice of these first two steps has been very successful. So far, we have knocked on the doors of more than one hundred thousand homes, baptized more than six thousand people, and set up approximately one thousand nine hundred home meetings with more than three thousand people meeting regularly. In other words, of the newly baptized ones, more than half are meeting regularly in the homes. On the one hand, this proves that the new way is workable, and on the other hand, it shows us how great the need is. Now the churches in all the localities are rising up to coordinate and receive training in the new way. This will meet the need considerably.

After the successful practice of the first two steps of the new way, we must go on to the third step, which is to lead the new ones in the home meetings to advance in the truth and to grow in life. This is not just nourishing but teaching. Because this step affects the constitution of the entire church life, its importance is evident. Leading a big meeting or a training is not a problem for us because for many years we already have had much experience. When we speak of leading the home meetings, however, I am afraid that we do not know what to do. Although the principles are the same for both big meetings and small meetings, the practices which we learned in the past can easily be used to take care of the big meetings but are very inadequate to take care of the weekly home meetings. Therefore, we need to learn and spend much time in the study of how to successfully take the third step of the new way.

With respect to the fourth step, we hope that after six months of teaching in life and truth, we can care for and perfect the new ones to truly, practically, and fully have the church life. In other words, the fourth step is to bring the new ones into the full knowledge of the church, that they would intrinsically know what the church is and enter into the practical church life. By that time, the church life will be completely built up in the homes. This is our goal.

PREPARATION FOR LEADING AND CARING
FOR THE HOME MEETINGS

Receiving a Definite Burden from the Lord

There are a few things we must learn before we go to lead the home meetings. First, the saints raised up in the localities must have a clear burden from the Lord to consecrate two or three hours every week to Him. This time is not for empty running or aimless working, but for definitely going to lead and care for two home meetings, spending less than one hour in each home. Each home meeting should, at the most, last for fifty minutes; we must learn to be economical in our use of time.

In the past the big meetings choked the service of the saints, disabling their spirit for service and preventing the release of their desire to serve. Now the practice of the new way gives us an outlet. Unless we do not have a heart to serve, the six thousand new saints in two thousand households are a good opportunity for us to learn how to serve. We must pick up the burden in a definite way and not in a way that is careless or without much consideration. We must have a willing heart to really learn how to do this.

I hope that the full-time trainees would take the lead and help all the saints in the churches who have a serving heart to take the proper way. The trainees' function is to lead the saints and not to replace them. The saints should, on the one hand, follow the trainees to learn something and, on the other hand, follow the Lord's leading to receive a burden from Him to take care of two specific home meetings. Once the saints have received the burden, they should not carry out this burden half-way or in an inconsistent manner. They must go again and again to nourish and care for the new ones to such an extent that they understand and are completely sure about the new ones' situation so that they know how to bring them on.

Furthermore, the elders must be careful to not constantly change those who lead or take care of a home meeting. Otherwise, this will be like changing a child's nursing mother so frequently that the child loses its sense of security and has a hard time growing normally. Just as children need a sense of security, a home meeting also needs a sense of stability, so that the new ones will feel they can trust the church and be willing to receive its leading to go on. We all love the Lord, have a heart to serve Him, and are willing to consecrate two or three hours. Therefore, we should solemnly receive the burden from the Lord to lead and care for the new ones just as we lead and care for our children. Actually, they are our children. We should pray for them and care for everything about them. This is the first matter of our preparation.

Learning to Nourish as a Mother and Lead as a Father

Second, we must learn to nourish. When we go to lead a home meeting, we are not just attending a meeting but are leading and taking care of the new ones. In other words, they are our children, so we must feed and nurse them as a mother and also teach and exhort them as a father. We must bear all their problems. Some might refuse to do this, saying, "I cannot bear the problems even in my own family, so how can I bear the problems of two other families?" I dare not speak about any other matter, but concerning this matter I have much experience. When I was young, the Lord uprooted me from the world and gave me a heavy burden every day. It has been fifty-four years now. We may think that we would be able to relax if we could lay our burden down, but we are wrong. If we reject the Lord's burden, then Satan, the king of the world, will put his burden on us. If you ask me what you should do, my answer is this: The Lord is the way. You should go to Him to seek and rely on Him.

Furthermore, the more burdens we receive from the Lord, the more blessings we will have. When our burdens are gone, the Lord's blessing will stop. Two years ago there were more than six hundred churches in the Lord's recovery around the world. Now we have increased to almost nine hundred. This is the Lord's blessing. In the past three months we have gained six thousand people through our door-knocking and have established two thousand home meetings. This, too, is the Lord's blessing. Thus, when the Lord gives us a burden, He also gives us a blessing. The question is whether or not we are willing to receive the burden. When we receive the Lord's burden, we will also receive His blessing. If we wish to not be busy, to have no burdens, or to spend our days in a leisurely way, then we will live our days without the Lord's blessing. Our attitude should be that we are not afraid of being busy. We only fear not having "children." Bearing children is a heavy burden, yet it also brings much blessing. Therefore, we should not be afraid; rather, we should pick up the burden to care for our "children."

Practically Caring for the Needs of the New Ones

Third, we must practically care for the needs of the new ones. In the past we did not place much emphasis on such things as the so-called healing of the sick and casting out of demons; however, these things are definitely in the Bible. Sometimes when we go out to preach the gospel and lead people to be saved and baptized, some of them will have this kind of need, and we should care for them in these matters. There is no need for us to go out purposely to do these things, nor should we be too passive, but always seeking the so-called leading. The principle of the matter lies with "whenever." Whenever someone has a demon, we should cast the demon out; whenever someone is sick, we should heal him. Do not be afraid when you meet a demon. You should just cast him out boldly. When you meet with illness, do not be worried, just lay your hands on the sick one and pray, seeking the Lord's leading to heal the sick one. The Bible clearly says that the Lord bore our sicknesses and carried our sorrows (Isa. 53:4-5; Matt. 8:17). He is our great Physician, who is able to heal all our illnesses. Whenever we meet people with these needs, we should do these things to serve them. Although it is wrong to care just for these things, it is also a shortcoming and a mistake to intentionally avoid doing them.

Learning to Become the Right Kind of Person

Fourth, when we go to lead the home meetings, we ourselves first must be the kind of person that we want them to be. This means that if we lead the new ones to read the Bible

and pray, yet we ourselves do not have the habit of reading
the Bible and praying, then that is not acceptable. We cannot
lead others to read the Bible and pray unless we ourselves do
so. In the same way, how can we lead and exhort others to
forsake the world if we ourselves love the world? If we tell
new ones that the Lord today is the life-giving Spirit within
them and that they should follow Him—the Spirit—in their
spirit, then we ourselves must be such people—those who live
in the spirit every day and walk according to the Spirit. This
is not just a matter of practicing what we preach or of being a
pattern; instead, it is that we ourselves are such people in our
constitution. We love the Lord, fellowship with Him, long for
His Word, enjoy praying, obey the Spirit, walk according to
the Spirit, forsake the world as if it were dung, and live
wholly for the Lord. If we are such people when we go to lead
and care for a home meeting, then after a short while, we will
produce a great effect on the new ones.

New believers, especially young people, really like to
imitate spiritual people. When I was first saved, I saw an old
pastor whom I really admired in my heart, so I imitated his
every move and action. My sister studied theology in Nanking.
When she returned, she told me that at the seminary she met
many spiritual people who pursued the Lord. They all spoke
gently and elegantly, walked slowly with a Bible in their
hands, and after walking a few steps they would look up to
heaven. By nature I am a quick, impatient, and impulsive
person. After hearing my sister's fellowship, I wanted to learn
to speak cautiously and walk slowly. This illustrates how
every saved one wants to imitate the good pattern of spiritual
people. As long as we are proper people, when we go to visit
two households for forty to fifty minutes every week, we will
have a great influence on them. They might not say anything,
but unconsciously they will be affected and will even pay
attention to and imitate our way of dressing.

The most important thing in leading a meeting is our
person; people bear children who are just like themselves. We
learn Chinese ethical education from the time we are small,
not according to how much our parents teach us but mainly
according to what kind of pattern they show us. They live

altogether according to the Chinese ethical teachings, so they unconsciously plant those things into us until it even becomes very hard for us to change ourselves. Therefore, I exhort the brothers and sisters that since they have picked up the burden to lead the home meetings, they must pray earnestly before the Lord for the new ones and also consider their own condition to see whether they are the right people. We should not merely have a heart. We must also, more importantly, be right, and we must be the kind of person we want the new ones to be.

Taking the Lead but Not Being the Head

Fifth, when we take the lead, we must definitely not take it upon ourselves to be the head and do everything by ourselves. We may do this in the big meetings but definitely not in the home meetings. The home meetings do not have a specific person as the head. Therefore, although we go to lead the meetings, we must take a firm stand and let the new ones know that we are just meeting and participating together with them. This is just as if we were playing ball; we play together with them instead of just being a coach to teach them how to play without playing ourselves. Of course, we are more experienced, so sometimes when they do not know how to go on, we must "coach" them at the right time by asking them to sing, read the Bible, pray, or testify. We must always remember, however, to give the meeting to them. In this way, they will learn how to meet after just a few meetings and will be able to function in the home meetings.

I repeat, when you lead the home meetings, you absolutely must not have the attitude that you have the approval from the church to go to the home meetings as a teacher, coach, or head. If you go with such an attitude, the home meetings will be killed. You certainly must learn to meet with them and to bring them on as you meet. At the same time you must be careful not to bring the atmosphere of the big meetings into the home meetings. Big meetings should be carried out in an orderly manner. In contrast, home meetings are characterized by their disorderliness, and it does not matter even if the meetings drag on a little. We really must learn to meet with the new ones just like a family and talk about things together, leading and helping them as the need arises but without replacing them. Of course, we certainly must pay attention to the time and avoid meeting for too long.

Learning to Sing Hymns

Sixth, we must learn to sing hymns properly. Because in the past we have not paid much attention to music, the brothers and sisters have been affected and are not able to sing very well. I hope, however, that you would give more effort to learn to sing. When you go to visit new ones, it is best to bring the *100 Selected Hymns,* which contains hymns chosen out of all our hymns. We do not want to just learn the hymns ourselves; we must also teach the new ones to sing. Every time we go to see them we should teach them a hymn. We must teach the children especially, because they learn quickly. The content of the *100 Selected Hymns* is rich, so while we sing, we spontaneously teach them certain truths. Thus, we must diligently learn and teach the hymns.

Teaching the Truth

Seventh, we must teach the truth. When we lead the home meetings, the hardest point, which is also the most important matter, is teaching the truth. If we do not teach the truth, the home meetings will not have a center or a foundation. All the points mentioned above are peripheral matters as a preparation. The central point is to work the truth into people. This is very important. The materials concerning the truth among us are plentiful, especially the *Truth Lessons,* the content of which is particularly suited for use in the home meetings. We still feel, however, that the content of this book is somewhat difficult and a bit too weighty. This is why I encourage the teachers as soon as possible to select some lessons from the *Truth Lessons,* beginning with the experience of salvation, and compile them into suitable teaching materials to meet the needs of the home meetings.

In the same principle, when we go to teach the truth, we should not consider ourselves teachers. We go to teach, but we are not teachers. The way we teach is to read things with them. We want to give them the impression that we are also students and that at most we are students just a grade or two ahead of them who are learning the truth together with them. Before the home meetings, however, we must first study the message thoroughly and understand its content. Then when we read it together with them, we should not be inflexible but rather use all kinds of ways to read it. First, we must point out the important items and not fear repetition. In this way, we will always give them a deep impression. At the same time, when we read a portion that is full of inspiration, we can also ask them to give testimonies at any time, or to express their feelings and share something of the light and revelation which they themselves have touched.

The Content of the Meetings Needing to Be Living

Eighth, the content of the meetings must be living. The greatest lack among us is that when we read messages, we are very rigid and not at all living. When we read, at any time we should add prayer and the singing of hymns. We can also give testimonies, share our feelings, or fellowship some light at any time. We should not read on and on until people begin to nod off. If we use the way of fellowship, then we will be free and living. For example, when we read about being released, we can sing the hymn "Glorious freedom, wonderful freedom!" (*Hymns*, #310). In this way, the home meetings will be living and enlivening. Everyone will have such a good taste that they will look forward to the next meeting.

Some people may say, "We are not like the full-time serving ones, who specialize in these matters and have time to prepare thoroughly. We have our occupations, so how can we have as much energy as they have?" Yet the Bible shows us that all God's children have only one occupation, that is, being a Christian. Not only the full-time serving ones but all of us are in this unique occupation. As long as we all have a heart to learn and practice, then we will spontaneously be able to lead the home meetings. This does not require eloquence or a special gift. This is especially the case because we are always learning, so it does not matter if we do make a mistake. Therefore, as long as we are willing to learn and practice, we will ultimately learn the secret.

I would like to encourage the older saints to not consider themselves too old to learn and practice. I am as old as you are. If we consider ourselves old and tired, then we will not want to walk or move, so we will certainly fall ill in a short time. Even though we old people struggle and fight just to live, the more we move, the stronger we are. Therefore, we should all practice going out because this is beneficial to us. If the entire church would pick up the burden for the home meetings and go out to care for others, we will not only be able to meet a huge need but will also make the church full of vitality.

CONCLUSION

In conclusion, if the church is to grow and prosper until it arrives at the condition of the early church in the Bible, in which saved ones were added to the church day by day, then we absolutely must bring the church life into the homes. In the past, because we had a hard time breaking away from the influence of Christianity, we did not pay much attention to the form of our meetings. As a result, we were slow in our multiplication and increase. Today, however, the Lord has shown us a way in the Bible. What we need to do now is to endeavor to go on according to this new way and do our best to bring the church life into the homes. This is very crucial.

In our actual practice we must go out to lead the home meetings every week. After three months we can conclude our taking the lead and try to allow the new ones to take the lead themselves. But during those first three months we must lead and teach them, causing them to learn and practice until they are able to do what we do. Now there are already some new ones who have been through this perfecting and who are going out door-knocking with us. Some even have the heart to attend the full-time training. This is a very good sign. I hope that after these next three months, we will be able to let go of taking the lead in the meetings. This does not mean, however, that we stop going to them. We still must go, but the new ones themselves must take the lead. We will go on this way until we have met with them for a total of six months. Then they can completely "graduate," and the church life will be entirely in the homes of the new ones, ensuring that the home of every new one has the normal church life and that every new one can practically bear the responsibility of the church life.

Some might wonder how it can go this fast. Yes, this can truly go this fast. We need to turn our concepts. In the past our knowledge was inadequate, but now we are in an age of advancement and the standard of education has been raised. We must believe that the level of the new ones is also higher. In the past we felt that it was too hard to understand certain hymns, but now the new ones understand the hymns as soon as they sing them. Therefore, when we teach the new ones, we should not think that they will not be able to understand and therefore consider waiting until another time to tell them about certain things. We must realize that once we wait, we might end up waiting forever. We should just speak boldly and believe that they certainly are able to understand. Parents all know that the way to teach little children to speak is to constantly speak when you are around them. After you have spoken much, they spontaneously are able to speak too. If you do not teach them to speak, in just three years' time they become mutes who truly are not able to speak. Leading the home meetings is just like this. Do not be afraid to speak about the deeper truths such as the dispensing of the Triune God, God's economy, and the great mystery of Christ and the church. You must believe that by your speaking again and again, they will be able not only to understand but also to speak according to your speaking.

This time when I returned to Taiwan, I made a special trip to a barber shop that I used to frequent thirty years ago. I discovered that the barbers have changed their speaking. Their conversations are much higher and better than I had expected. This is because society has made progress. The barbers hear and see this progress every day, so spontaneously, their speaking also changes. Thus, when we go to the home meetings, we must also speak the high, deep truths until these high, deep truths become part of the ordinary conversation among us.

CHAPTER SEVEN

THE KEY TO THE SUCCESS OF THE NEW WAY

SOME INSTRUCTIONS CONCERNING
THE FURTHERANCE OF THE NEW WAY

There are a few matters which we must be clear about in the practice of the new way. First, the church in Taipei is taking the lead in this matter. Although at present it has not fully entered in, at least it has begun. Second, the results from this term of the training have been very rich: six thousand were baptized through door-knocking and two thousand home meetings have been established. At present there are seven hundred trainees who are still bearing this burden. Third, we have a long-range view before us, which is the evangelization of Taiwan and then of the world.

We pointed out previously that we will need five years to complete the evangelization of Taiwan and that the ideal situation would be to produce one thousand full-time serving ones. Now there are about five hundred qualified full-time trainees; if in the next year and the following year we are able to produce another two hundred fifty trainees per year, we will have a total of one thousand. If this happens, the goal of evangelizing Taiwan in five years will be assured. This future, this long-range view, is set before us, so we must not slow down or stop; instead, we must continue pressing on.

Since 1974 we have had the summer and winter trainings for the life-study of the Bible. On average, more than eighteen hundred people attend the live training, and together with the video trainings there are a total of at least five thousand people attending every training. This burden is necessary and very heavy. Now the full-time training here in Taipei is burning like wildfire, but I must return to America to prepare for the life-study training. Therefore, I hope that the trainers will be able to continue bearing this heavy burden to keep the training moving forward.

Apart from the trainers, I hope that three other groups in the churches would be able to offer their shoulders to help bear the burden of the practice of the Lord's new way. The first group is the elders in the church in Taipei. Ephesians 5:14 says, "Awake, sleeper." We cannot continue sleeping; we must awake and arise. Ninety elders take the lead in twenty-three meeting halls to promote the new way for the Lord's recovery. This burden is very heavy. If the changing of the system is delayed due to the elders' unwillingness to rise up, we may not know its effect until eternity. This is a great matter. The new way must get through first in the church in Taipei. If the elders in Taipei do not wake up, then the church in Taipei will be like a "dead end," and it will drain the morale out of the training. I hope the elders in the church in Taipei will all see this crucial point.

The second group is the ones who have the heart to remain in the full-time training. There are a total of about five hundred from abroad, from other places in this province, and from the city of Taipei itself who are willing to stay and help care for the two thousand home meetings. Among these are about one hundred saints from abroad, many of whom want to bring their families over to Taiwan. There are also many from overseas who want to attend the next term of the training. The church in Taipei must prepare places for them to live; this burden is also very heavy.

The third group is all the saints from the church in Taipei who, two weeks ago, signed their names to consecrate themselves and express their willingness to go out door-knocking for two hours every week for the Lord or to lead a home meeting. We need to have some fellowship with these three groups of people to instruct them and give them some explanation so that they will understand what they should do in the present situation.

A CRUCIAL STEP FOR PRACTICING THE NEW WAY

We have said that we must lead the home meetings properly

so that the new ones will know the truth and grow in life. This is the third step of the actual practice of the new way, and it is a very important and crucial step. The success or failure of the new way completely hinges on whether or not we are able to carry out and get through this step. We now have more than six thousand newly baptized ones and have set up two thousand home meetings, so it is just as if we have given birth to the babies and have set up a good environment to care for them. Therefore, the next step is to determine how we will actually nurture and care for them.

Now that so much progress has been made in medicine, many premature babies can be raised to maturity. I have a grandson who was only as big as a little frog when he was born. When I saw him, I doubted whether he would be able to grow up, but now he is tall and husky and plays football very well with the American children. This is because his mother did a good job of feeding and caring for him. In the same way, today when we gain people through door-knocking and establish meetings in their homes, if we do not have the proper way to feed them, they will all die prematurely in about three months. Therefore, the way in which we lead and care for people will determine whether this new way for the Lord's recovery will succeed and prosper in bringing the Lord's recovery on, or whether this way will be a "dead end" which will cause us to "close shop." Some may ask why we must take the new way. First, the new way is according to the Bible. Second, a review of the past thirty years of history in Taiwan shows that the lack of home meetings as a support is the reason that many were baptized but few have remained. We have also heard many testimonies from the trainees who have gone out and knocked on the doors of many dormant saints who have not been in meetings for a long time. We have had this question in our heart for a long time: over the years we have baptized more than 100,000, but where did all those people go? Five years ago there were three hundred meeting in hall one in the church in Taipei, now there are still three hundred, and I am afraid that by the end of the world, there will still be three hundred. Why is this? It is because there are no home meetings as the supporting foundation. Now the practice of the new way is making the home the focal point, so it gives us all a supporting foundation.

It is very easy to see that without a good church life, there is no way to retain people. If we use a hose to pump water out of a well and onto the ground, the water will soon seep back into its original place. The result is that while we are pumping water on the one hand and pouring water on the other, the water is simultaneously seeping back into the ground. Unless we have a container, we will not be able to keep the water from leaking away. The church life should be like a reservoir which keeps the water from leaking away whenever it rains, because the water is completely stored up in the reservoir. It is not easy to build a large reservoir, but it is very easy to find water pots. Each home meeting, even if it cannot be considered a small reservoir, can be considered a small water pot. The water which we pump up can be poured into these pots. From the beginning to the end of the year, only a small amount will leak out. For the most part the water can be stored up. In the past our failure was that we only had the big meetings and did not build up the home meetings, so we did not have a place to store the water. It was like giving birth to children with no place to raise them. Now we have found that the home meetings are the right place for the new ones to grow up and live. Therefore, we all must see clearly that the new way depends on the home meetings, and the home meetings depend on how we lead and perfect the new ones.

THE PRACTICAL COORDINATION OF THE CHURCH

The fourth practical step for the practice of the new way is to lead the new ones, who have been baptized, who have home meetings established in their homes, and who have been led to know the truth and pursue the growth in life, into the full knowledge of the church and into the practical church life. This step very much requires the coordination of the local church. This means that although the saints raised up by the local church have helped in door-knocking and in caring for home meetings, the new ones that they gain cannot remain only in the home meetings but need to be brought into the church life. Therefore, the church must have a church life which is up to the standard in order to support these new ones for this further step. To illustrate, we may have a large reservoir with water flowing in constantly; however, if the reservoir has a breach or a hole, then the water will eventually all run out. After a rainstorm the reservoir may be full, but after just half a month the water will all run out through the breach or the hole. This is the root of the problem. Therefore, in order to bring new ones into the practical church life, the church must rise up to coordinate without any breaches or leaky holes so that we will not lose the water which is flowing in.

The Church Meetings

The first matter in which the church must coordinate is the church meetings. The church meetings must be living, fresh, moving, and rich. If the meetings are like this, not only the new ones but also anyone who comes will be supplied and touched. If the church meetings are neither hot nor cold, neither high nor low, and if everyone does not function, but instead just a few leading, responsible brothers bear the entire meeting, then the meeting will be dull and tasteless. This will have a great effect on the new ones.

In some Lord's table meetings, the elders work very hard to pray again and again, sometimes praying at least five or six times, because not many other people pray. Thus, the meetings are not living, moving, fresh, or rich. The new ones which we have now gained through door-knocking are mostly very fresh and hungry. As soon as we bring them into the present condition of the church meetings, the meetings might dampen their interest and be unable to meet their needs. Some people may even receive a negative impression. Some new ones have been helped very much by the home meetings, but after they are brought to the larger church meetings, they do not want to come again because the big meetings cannot meet their need and taste.

The Elders' Responsibility

For this reason, the elders must understand the seriousness of this matter and do their best to rise up and bear this important and great responsibility of bringing the saints into a living, fresh enjoyment for the success of the practice of the new way. We have already been quite successful in gaining new ones through door-knocking and in establishing home meetings. After this, we need to find a way to uphold the new ones, and the key to this is with the elders.

The world-famous American evangelist, Billy Graham, began to serve the Lord in Los Angeles in 1949. He also saw that in many of his large gospel meetings more than ten thousand people would leave their names. After sending them to all the denominations, however, most of them became very cold and were never heard from again. Today the situation in the Lord's recovery is somewhat like this. Therefore, the churches must rise up to coordinate with the move of the Lord's new way. If the churches are to rise up, the greatest responsibility falls upon the elders. They cannot just oversee others taking the new way while they themselves do not move. In the local church life the elders are the first "link," the leading sheep who take the lead in the flock. If they do not go or move, the flock behind them will not be able to move or go on at all. The influence of the leading sheep is very great.

In 1958 I visited England, and the brothers there made a special trip to take me to a sheep ranch in Scotland to see how the flocks of sheep move. The flock is totally dependent on the leading of the head sheep. If the head sheep bleats, the entire flock bleats. If the head sheep lies down, the entire flock lies down. If the head sheep stops walking, the entire flock stops moving, and no matter how much you prod them, they will not move again until you get to the head sheep and force it to move. The Lord's Word says very clearly that the church is God's flock and the elders are the leading sheep who lead the entire flock (Acts 20:28-29; 1 Pet. 5:2-3). If the elders take the lead not to move, then how can the saints move?

We must keep looking to the Lord for His care, especially the elders. They need to fast and pray once a week, asking the Lord to care for the saints and to bring them into the vision and practice of the new way. This practice has already involved over a thousand people and has incurred great expense. However, the Lord has had mercy on us and has completely met our every need by His rich supply. Now the responsibility for this great move has been transferred to the elders of the church in Taipei. If this "first link"—the elders—does not move, then all our previous efforts will be nullified. Therefore, I hope that the elders will be touched to rise up and move so that the new way will reach the entire church through them.

Furthermore, the elders should not be elders in name only, nor should the eldership be an empty position. According to the Bible, the elders should shepherd the flock by becoming patterns to the flock. Therefore, if the elders do not take action, the saints have no way to grow up, and the church has no way to go on. Hence, all the saints, all those who love the Lord, who love the Lord's recovery, and who love the Lord's churches, should receive a burden to pray for the church in Taipei, particularly for the elders, calling on the Lord to raise them up and push them forward. If, as the crucial "first link," they cannot get through or take action, then all our previous efforts in changing the system will be nullified, and we will not be able to get through in the matter of the new way.

Bringing the New Ones into the Church Life

When we go out to lead the home meetings, teach the truth to the new ones, and lead them to grow in life, there will be a necessary process. The working out of this process will not be uniform; some new ones will learn a little faster, while others will go somewhat more slowly. For example, some will be eager to learn what the church is, so we should take advantage of the opportunity to stir up their love for the Lord and the church and bring them to the church meetings. We must, however, pay attention to the matter of bringing them to the appropriate meetings. Otherwise, not only will we be unable to help them, but we may even damage them. This is why we say that the local churches must coordinate in the matter of the meetings by making them living, fresh, and full of supply. Other new ones may be reluctant to leave the home meetings and may even be unwilling to meet in the homes of other people. Concerning these ones, we should still spend time to care for them, feeding and supplying them wisely until we can bring them out of their homes.

The local churches are not perfect. Although it seems that we are entrusting the elders of the church in Taipei with the responsibility of the success or failure of the new way, actually it is the responsibility of the elders in all the local churches also. The reason Paul wrote so many epistles to so many local churches, such as the church in Rome, the church in Corinth, and the church in Ephesus, was that every local church needed perfecting. The saints leading the home meetings also need the wisdom to determine the situation of the new ones; if they are mature, they should be brought to attend the appropriate church meetings. This requires us to have much learning.

Forming the Home Meetings into Group Meetings and Eventually Leading the New Ones to the Lord's Day Meetings

During this time of transition, if we are faithful, the home meetings can be formed—not formally or organizationally, but spontaneously—into group meetings. For example, according to the practical situation, you may ask several neighboring homes which are under your care to gather together and have a small group meeting every once in awhile. This can be likened to piling burning coals together: the more you pile them up, the brighter the fire burns. These three to five homes which come together will slowly get to know one another, and as they become familiar with each other, they will gradually learn to like one another. Then they will be able to stir up their love and encourage one another. We should not allow the new ones to remain just in the home meetings, or we will be like mothers who keep their children at home and do not let them leave to get an education. This makes it very difficult for them to grow well. The goal of leading the home meetings is to bring a few homes together to gradually make them a group meeting and ultimately to bring the new ones into the church so that they may have a proper church life. Thus, the church meetings must be living, fresh, rich, moving, and full of supply so that the saints will feel confident that they can bring the new ones.

FURTHERING THE LORD'S RECOVERY
BY PRACTICING THE NEW WAY

According to the statistics, the rate of increase in Christianity over the past twenty years has been very low, while the rate of increase for other religions like Buddhism or Islam has been very high. The reason is that the system in Christianity is wrong, because all the believers do nothing with the hired pastors doing everything for them. This kind of practice cannot cause the believers to live and grow; instead, it kills them and nullifies their organic function. One of the earliest Christian denominations which came to Taiwan was the Scottish Presbyterian Church; it has a history of over one hundred years here, but at present they have only a little over 100,000 members. The local churches are next with only forty or fifty thousand; the third is the True Jesus Church with twenty or thirty thousand. These three added together make only about 200,000, so when we include the other Christian groups, the total number of Christians in Taiwan is only about 500,000. This fact is very disappointing.

Not only has the situation in Christianity become disheartening; even the so-called churches in the Lord's recovery have fallen and gone backwards into a condition that is about the same as that of Christianity. In 1949 we began the work in Taiwan, and in the first four or five years the numbers kept increasing from four or five hundred all the way up to 40,000 or 50,000. After almost forty years, the present number is still about 40,000 or 50,000. What is the reason for this? It must be that the practice of having big meetings in which one person speaks and everyone else listens is killing the organic function of the saints while at the same time it is killing the increase and spread of the churches.

However, due to God's faithfulness, we are not discouraged, and within us there is a long-range view that home meeting after home meeting will be raised up until each home meeting is full of vitality and everyone—male, female, young, and old—can speak, sing, and function. We must accomplish this in the shortest time possible, so that every home meeting will be living and functioning. Then when we go out door-knocking to preach the gospel, we will bring people to salvation without having to rely on preachers. Instead, household after household will go out, and one household will perfect another household. Then the rate of increase will be extremely high.

It may be that we all are accustomed to the big meetings and big façades. The older saints especially think it is very good to come to a big meeting and see at least three hundred or five hundred people sitting there with at least one person who knows how to preach. They wonder why it is necessary to break these big meetings up into meetings of only three or five people in which everyone must speak and take the lead even if they do not know how to do these things. In their opinion these meetings are not very orderly or beautiful. However, the Lord is not interested in a façade. He only cares whether or not His children are functioning. If we can lead 20,000 home meetings with 50,000 or 60,000 new ones, it will be very easy for them to go out door-knocking. Today the neighborhoods are all composed of high-rise buildings. If the Lord has mercy on us, we can get ten percent of the households in every high-rise building to be saved. Then they can go out door-knocking and preach the gospel to the other ninety percent of the families. It would be so easy because they would all know one another. This is not being idealistic. Rather, this is a practical, long-range view set before us. May the Lord have mercy on us that we would be able to carry out this long-range view and testify that this is the Lord's recovery and the Lord's church.

This does not mean, however, that the big meetings do not have their function. Actually, for the enjoyment of the riches of the Body, we need to have combined meetings of the entire church at least six times a year, two of which should be the graduation meetings of the full-time training. Then we should have some joyful gatherings as feasts once every three months.

THE STRUCTURE OF THE CHURCH MEETINGS

In between the group meetings and the meetings in the

meeting halls, we may need yet another level of meetings. Taipei has a few districts with six or seven hundred saints and some with three or four hundred saints. In these districts, we should have a meeting place to allow these saints to have a meeting that is nearby, in which they can help one another. Even if they cannot all come, at least a good number can come. The subduing strength of such a district meeting will greatly influence the entire community.

In conclusion, the meetings of the church can be divided into at least five levels: home meetings, group meetings, district meetings, meeting-hall meetings, and big joint meetings. We should have these five levels of meetings regularly, but we must have the home meetings as the foundation. If the home meetings are not done well, nothing else will be profitable. This will require the elders to take the lead personally and all the brothers and sisters to follow in coordination with the help of the full-time trainees. Then we will certainly produce a good result quickly. This is the long-range view for which we are hoping. I believe that in a few years this will be seen by the angels, the devil, the worldly people, and Christianity. This is the Lord's church in which there is no organization or dependence on preachers, but in which all are living and following the Lord's leading. Even the question of whether to continue as a full-time serving one or to get a job is completely organic and free.

The first two steps of the new way have been put into effective practice; the last two steps need further research. Although we already have a rough framework and road for the last two steps, we still need the detailed research and experiments, especially concerning how to lead the home meetings, teach the truth, and minister life. On the one hand, we need to research, and on the other hand, we must continue going on, or else our research will not have a foundation, and there will be a blow to our morale.

THREE IMPORTANT MATTERS RELATED TO THE MOVE OF THE ENTIRE CHURCH

Related to the ministry, we have been led by the Lord to work with the goal of building up the church. Therefore, there are three important matters that we must fellowship about so that all the churches will know the present situation of our work. First, we have bought more than twenty-four acres of land in Linkou, and we hope to be able to build a large meeting hall, but our application for the building permit was not approved. Now we are busy carrying out the training and researching the new way; when we want to have a big meeting, we can rent a stadium. From this perspective, the matter of building the large meeting hall in Linkou can be postponed without interrupting our work.

Second, there is the matter of the support for the full-time serving ones. In order to evangelize Taiwan, it would be best if there were 2,500 full-time serving ones; at least we will need one thousand. If we calculate for one thousand, to support their living and to meet the need of their activities, we will need at least NT$10 million every month, so in one year we will need NT$120 million. If we calculate that in US dollars it would be about $4 million. This is not a light burden. Therefore, there is the need for us to take practical action by offering with respect to manpower, time, and money. Without people, time, or money, we will not be able to do anything. I hope that all the elders will have thorough fellowship with all the saints concerning this need.

Up to now there are not yet that many full-time serving ones. The Lord's grace, however, is always rich and overflowing, so we still do not feel straitened. But once the spreading work officially begins, our financial needs will increase greatly, and if at that time we cannot keep up with the financial needs, it will affect the morale and create problems. In the present stage all the churches, not only in Taiwan but over the whole earth, should care for this matter in one accord and participate in this great move of the Lord in Taiwan. This will not end in a short time but will continue on for at least five years. For this reason we all should properly receive this burden before the Lord to faithfully offer our portion. If we do this, the situation will get broader and wider, and the increase of the Lord's grace will follow.

Third, there is the need of the full-time training. Because this is a world-wide training, many saints from overseas are attending. The cost of their travel alone is a very great expense. In the future there will also be a training in America which will be for the saints from the Western Hemisphere, while the training in Taiwan will mainly be for the saints from the Far East. At present, we do not have enough helpers, our preparation is not adequate, and the practical way for the carrying out of the training has not yet been made clear. As a result we can only have a training here in Taiwan. This requires not only some arrangements in the affairs of personnel but also a large financial supply, so we all must spare no effort.

Communications today are increasingly improving, so the globe has become smaller. Therefore, the Lord's work is spreading more and more. Moreover, English has become the world language, and the Lord has arranged that America and Taiwan would be the two main training centers for the move of His recovery. This is truly the Lord's grace, so we must grasp it. Three years ago there were a total of just over six hundred churches in the entire world, but now we have already increased to about nine hundred localities. Most of these are located in Central and South America. There are also some in Europe. All of this requires our coordination through the training and financial supply. Otherwise, we will not be able to keep up with the Lord's move.

Hence, we all must receive the burden not just for Taiwan and the Far East but also for the entire earth. May we all have a clear understanding of the present move among the churches in the Lord's recovery, and may we know the long-range view for the work, as well as for our future plans, so that we will be able to practically coordinate with the Lord and really participate in His present move.

About the Author

Witness Lee was born in 1905 in northern China and raised in a Christian family. At age 19 he was fully captured for Christ and immediately consecrated himself to preach the gospel for the rest of his life. Early in his service, he met Watchman Nee, a renowned preacher, teacher, and writer. Witness Lee labored together with Watchman Nee under his direction. In 1934 Watchman Nee entrusted Witness Lee with the responsibility for his publication operation, called the Shanghai Gospel Bookroom.

Prior to the Communist takeover in 1949, Witness Lee was sent by Watchman Nee and his other co-workers to Taiwan to insure that the things delivered to them by the Lord would not be lost. Watchman Nee instructed Witness Lee to continue the former's publishing operation abroad as the Taiwan Gospel Bookroom, which has been publicly recognized as the publisher of Watchman Nee's works outside China. Witness Lee's work in Taiwan manifested the Lord's abundant blessing. From a mere 350 believers, newly fled from the mainland, the churches in Taiwan grew to 20,000 in five years.

In 1962 Witness Lee felt led of the Lord to come to the United States, settling in California. During his 35 years of service in the U.S., he ministered in weekly meetings and weekend conferences, delivering several thousand spoken messages. Much of his speaking has since been published as over 400 titles. Many of these have been translated into over fourteen languages. He gave his last public conference in February 1997 at the age of 91.

He leaves behind a prolific presentation of the truth in the Bible. His major work, *Life-study of the Bible,* comprises over 25,000 pages of commentary on every book of the Bible from the perspective of the believers' enjoyment and experience of God's divine life in Christ through the Holy Spirit. Witness Lee was the chief editor of a new translation of the New Testament into Chinese called the Recovery Version and directed the translation of the same into English. The Recovery Version also appears in a number of other languages. He provided an extensive body of footnotes, outlines, and spiritual cross references. A radio broadcast of his messages can be heard on Christian radio stations in the United States. In 1965 Witness Lee founded Living Stream Ministry, a non-profit corporation, located in Anaheim, California, which officially presents his and Watchman Nee's ministry.

Witness Lee's ministry emphasizes the experience of Christ as life and the practical oneness of the believers as the Body of Christ. Stressing the importance of attending to both these matters, he led the churches under his care to grow in Christian life and function. He was unbending in his conviction that God's goal is not narrow sectarianism but the Body of Christ. In time, believers began to meet simply as the church in their localities in response to this conviction. In recent years a number of new churches have been raised up in Russia and in many eastern European countries.

OTHER BOOKS PUBLISHED BY
Living Stream Ministry

Titles by Witness Lee:

Abraham—Called by God	0-7363-0359-6
The Experience of Life	0-87083-417-7
The Knowledge of Life	0-87083-419-3
The Tree of Life	0-87083-300-6
The Economy of God	0-87083-415-0
The Divine Economy	0-87083-268-9
God's New Testament Economy	0-87083-199-2
The World Situation and God's Move	0-87083-092-9
Christ vs. Religion	0-87083-010-4
The All-inclusive Christ	0-87083-020-1
Gospel Outlines	0-87083-039-2
Character	0-87083-322-7
The Secret of Experiencing Christ	0-87083-227-1
The Life and Way for the Practice of the Church Life	0-87083-785-0
The Basic Revelation in the Holy Scriptures	0-87083-105-4
The Crucial Revelation of Life in the Scriptures	0-87083-372-3
The Spirit with Our Spirit	0-87083-798-2
Christ as the Reality	0-87083-047-3
The Central Line of the Divine Revelation	0-87083-960-8
The Full Knowledge of the Word of God	0-87083-289-1
Watchman Nee—A Seer of the Divine Revelation ...	0-87083-625-0

Titles by Watchman Nee:

How to Study the Bible	0-7363-0407-X
God's Overcomers	0-7363-0433-9
The New Covenant	0-7363-0088-0
The Spiritual Man 3 volumes	0-7363-0269-7
Authority and Submission	0-7363-0185-2
The Overcoming Life	1-57593-817-0
The Glorious Church	0-87083-745-1
The Prayer Ministry of the Church	0-87083-860-1
The Breaking of the Outer Man and the Release ...	1-57593-955-X
The Mystery of Christ	1-57593-954-1
The God of Abraham, Isaac, and Jacob	0-87083-932-2
The Song of Songs	0-87083-872-5
The Gospel of God 2 volumes	1-57593-953-3
The Normal Christian Church Life	0-87083-027-9
The Character of the Lord's Worker	1-57593-322-5
The Normal Christian Faith	0-87083-748-6
Watchman Nee's Testimony	0-87083-051-1

Available at
Christian bookstores, or contact Living Stream Ministry
2431 W. La Palma Ave. • Anaheim, CA 92801
1-800-549-5164 • www.livingstream.com